The Invisible Force Affecting Our Children

The Loveday Method
Part 2

The Second Book of a

Series of Seven Books.

A Heptalogy
by
Geoffrey Loveday

Every parent should take the time to read this book.

The Invisible Force Affecting Our Children – The Loveday Method Part 2

Author: Geoffrey Loveday

Copyright © 2023 by Geoffrey Loveday - All Rights Reserved.

The right of Geoffrey Loveday to be identified as author of this work has been asserted by the author in accordance with section 77 and 78 of the Copyright, Designs and Patents Act 1988.

First Published in 2023

ISBN 978-1-915996-01-5 (Paperback)
      978-1-915996-18-3 (Hardback)
      978-1-915996-19-0 (eBook)

Published by:
    Maple Publishers
    Fairbourne Drive, Atterbury,
    Milton Keynes,
    MK10 9RG, UK
    www.maplepublishers.com

A CIP catalogue record for this title is available from the British Library.

It is not legal to reproduce, duplicate, or transmit any part of this document in either electronic means or printed format. Recording of this publication is strictly prohibited.

Although the information in this book is intended to help you make better-informed decisions, it should not be used as a substitute for expert medical advice.

Users are free to use the information in this book however they choose.

The authors and publisher cannot be held responsible for any consequences that result from the usage of information in this book.

The author or the publisher assumes no responsibility or liability for how you use the information contained herein.

The author reiterates that throughout my book, I have drawn on the stories of the people I've helped. These people are real, but to protect their privacy, I have changed their names.

The results may vary from person to person.

I wonder where life will take us now...

And the journey begins.

Let me take you on this magical adventure.

Contents

Dedication: 7
Inspiration.. 9
Acknowledgement 11
A little about me... 12
Introduction.. 14
PART ONE 19
The Magical Forest... 20
Chapter 1: Fear of the Dark 23
Chapter 2: Lucy's Story 26
Chapter 3: Bullying 38
Chapter 4: Anxiety Disorders in Children 43
Chapter 5: Violence in the Home 46
Chapter 6: Danny's Story 49
Chapter 7: Yvonne's Story 53
Chapter 8: Nightmares... 56
Chapter 9: Jenny's Story 64
Chapter 10: A Journey with Brent 68
Chapter 11: Jane's Story 83
Chapter 12: Depression 88
Chapter 13: Tony's Story 90
Chapter 14: Diane's Story 96
Chapter 15: David's Magical Journey 101
Chapter 16: Amy's Story 110
Chapter 17: Jerry's Story 141

Chapter 18: James' Story 158

Chapter 19: Ryan's Journey. 180

PART TWO 199

Chapter 20: Transgenerational Trauma.............. 200

    Native North American tribes and Native Americans 202

    Chinese Culture 204

    African American.. 205

    Japanese Beliefs 206

    The Aeta 208

Chapter 21: The Loveday Method. 210

PART THREE.. 217

Chapter 22: An Unseen Influence 218

    Messages from Water 224

    Experiments with Rice and Water 228

    Dr Masaru Emoto 228

    Adam Mock 230

    Geoffrey Loveday 231

    The Power of Plants 242

    The Placebo Effect 245

    Kirlian Photography 251

    The Power of Belief 253

    The Power of the Mind 255

    Émile Coué 258

    Putting the Pieces Together 262

PART FOUR 265

Chapter 23: The Thirty-Day Challenge 266

Chapter 24: Sleep Hypnosis 267
　Hypnopaedia 267
　Sleep Hypnosis: Dave Elman 269
Chapter 25: Reprogramme the Child's Mind.........278
Chapter 26: The Loveday Method for Children.....282
　The Journey 285
　Conclusion 289
Bibliography 293

Dedication:

I want to dedicate this book to the children who are suffering in the world today. They are the ones who need our help the most, and I hope that through this book, we can all learn to stand up for them and fight for their rights.

How we educate our children can have a significant impact on the course their future takes. How we raise our children can have a significant effect on their future. The way we talk to them, the way we discipline them, and the way we show them love all play a role in shaping who they will become.

If we want our children to be kind and compassionate, we need to model that behaviour for them. If we want them to be successful in life, we need to instil a strong work ethic and a positive attitude.

The most important thing we can do for our children is to give them a foundation of love and security. When they know that they are loved unconditionally, they will be able to face the world with confidence.

Originally written for parents, this book is for both children and adults who are searching for help. You will realise how important it is that you should deal with the problem at an early age.

Inspiration

This book was written to inspire children to be stronger in their minds. The author believes that if children can learn to be mentally strong, they will be better equipped to handle the challenges life throws at them.

The book provides practical tips and advice on how to develop mental strength, such as setting goals and overcoming obstacles. It also includes inspiring stories of children who have faced difficult circumstances and come out stronger for it.

I hope that by reading this book, children will learn that they are capable of overcoming anything life throws at them. With mental strength, they can achieve anything they set their minds to.

The stories contained in this book are about individuals who have encountered challenging situations and emerged victorious. They are living proof that it is possible to make positive changes in one's life, even though problems may appear to be insurmountable.

I hope that hearing about their experiences would motivate you to never give up on yourself and to always keep moving forward no matter what.

And know where to get the help you may need.

Acknowledgement

I would like to thank the following people for their help in making this book possible:

First and foremost, I want to thank the children who were brave enough to share their stories with me. Without them, this book would not be possible.

I also want to thank their parents and guardians for entrusting me with their stories. I know it was not easy, but I hope that by sharing their experiences, we can make the world a better place for all children.

I would also like to thank Capt. Martin C. Sanderson for editing and proofreading and doing the finishing touches to the book to make it so easy to read.

I would want to take this opportunity to thank Larry Elman and Cheryl Modjoros-Elman for continuing the work that Dave Elman was able to achieve in his role as a hypnotist. Larry and Cheryl continue Dave Elman's legacy.

A little about me...

This is the part I hate. My name is Geoffrey Elliott Loveday. Mustn't forget my middle name. I hated it when I was a child. But as I got older, somehow it grew on me.

As long as I can remember I've always felt different people call me an old soul as though I'd been here before.

You know I think they could be right. I've always had a need to help people. I've always been searching for an answer, which led me to hypnosis. But something was missing with hypnotherapy, even today.

So I had to look deeper to find the answer to see why there are so many adults and children suffering in the world today.

I call it an invisible disease that is affecting our lives today.

When I did the research I realised these feelings that we have been holding onto were there before we were born. And that we are reliving someone else's life.

And so The Loveday Method was formed.

"The manner in which we educate our children can have a significant impact on the course their future takes."

Geoffrey. E. Loveday

Introduction

Inherited Therapy and The Loveday Method is one of my newest approaches to helping people overcome many of the problems and symptoms that are holding them back from living a happy and fulfilling life.

I am a full-time professional hypnotherapist and practitioner in pure–hypnoanalysis, as well as a Certified Hypnosis Instructor. And now, much to my surprise, the author of a book entitled:

Are You Reliving Someone Else's Life? The Loveday Method.

I find it difficult to talk about myself. This is what one of my clients had to say.

"When working with Geoff, you go on a journey. You won't know what you'll find until you see it, but don't worry. While our shadow is shy, it's a beautiful friend that will love you unconditionally if you let it. I can promise you that no matter what happens in your life, working with Geoff Loveday will be the best thing you do.

"I love and appreciate this man more than I could ever tell you! He WILL change your life in the way he's changed mine.

"Thank you, Geoff; I hope these words showcase your mastery in the light it deserves.

Mathew."

So why am I writing a second book? Originally I had it in my mind to write seven books. The seventh book was supposed to be about children.

One night, I woke up at about three in the morning, got up, went downstairs, switched the computer on and started writing. It's as if the universe wanted me to write again. And the first book, "Are You Reliving Someone else's Life?" wasn't even out yet.

So I started writing and I realised this book needed to be written. I decided to call it:

"The Invisible Force Affecting Our Children
The Loveday Method Part 2

Every parent should take the time to read this book."

Are our children suffering today as the result of our ancestors and the unhappiness they are feeling every day was there before they were born? And they are reliving someone else's life?

What do you think? Did it originate with them?

I know as a parent you feel the pain and suffering your children are going through and you are searching for help.

Where do you go for help; your doctor? They refer you to a psychiatrist, or counsellor, or prescribe a course of antidepressants.

Is this the answer?

Do you want your children to start life by being dependent on a drug that can affect them for the rest of their lives? Don't forget these drugs have side effects that can cause more harm than good, especially when trying to come off them.

Now, I am not saying that in certain cases they are not needed. But don't you think that, as a parent, you should find out if there is another solution that is safer for your child?

I know I would.

Is what I am saying guaranteed? Of course not. Do doctors give guarantees? Never. But just suppose one in ten children can be helped? And one of those that could be helped is your child.

Would it be worth it?

Of course, we as parents want our children to grow up healthy and have an amazing life.

I want you to think for a moment. Do the feelings they are going through originate with them? Is there someone in their family history that was going through the same emotions?

I cannot take credit for these questions. The original book was written by an extraordinary man with a vision.

"It Didn't Start With You", by Mark Wolynn.[1]

The answers you are searching for are in this book. Throughout my book, I have drawn on the stories of the children I've helped. The children are real, but to protect their privacy I have changed their names.

I am unbelievably grateful to the families and guardians for letting me share their stories and how, through hypnosis, they have been saved. Not only have they been saved, but together we've stopped future generations from following the same debilitating path.

"If you're going through hell, keep going."
Winston Churchill

---

[1] Wolynn, M., 2017. It Didn't Start with You. Penguin Publishing Group, p.125.

PART ONE

Their Stories.

The Magical Forest

"Once upon a time, in a land far away, there was a magical forest where the trees glowed with a gentle, shimmering light. It was said that the forest was enchanted and that it held the power to heal any troubled mind.

"One day, a little girl named Lily wandered into the enchanted forest. She had been feeling sad and anxious lately and she hoped that the magic of the forest could help ease her worries.

"As she walked deeper into the forest, the trees whispered to her, telling her that they could hear her thoughts and they were there to help. Suddenly, the ground beneath her feet began to glow, and a beautiful rainbow path appeared before her.

"Lily followed the rainbow path, and as she walked, she felt her worries and fears melting away. The colours of the rainbow seemed to wrap around her like a warm, comforting blanket, and she felt a sense of peace and calm wash over her.

"Finally, Lily came to a clearing in the centre of the forest, where a wise old owl was perched on a branch. The owl spoke to her in a gentle voice, telling her that she was strong and brave and that she had the power within her to overcome any challenge.

"Lily felt a surge of courage and confidence rise within her, and she knew that she could face anything that came her way. She thanked the wise old owl and the enchanted forest for their magic, and she walked back home feeling renewed and refreshed.

"From that day on, whenever Lily felt sad or anxious, she would close her eyes and imagine the rainbow path leading her back to the enchanted forest. She knew that the magic of the forest would always be there to heal her thoughts and lift her spirits and that she was never truly alone."

The story I've shared with you is an imaginative work of fiction, crafted to transport readers to fantastical worlds full of wonder and enchantment. Although they are not based on actual events, they explore important themes such as the power of the human mind and the significance of self-discovery.

While the magical elements of the stories are make-believe, they still contain valuable insights that can be relevant to real life. The tales encourage readers to ponder the potential of their own minds and consider how their thoughts and emotions can impact their overall well-being.

In essence, these stories may not be grounded in reality, but their messages can inspire us to delve deeper into our own minds and discover the transformative power within ourselves.

Chapter 1: Fear of the Dark

We look at our children and think they have no worries or fears, but what if one day they came to us and said they were afraid of the dark?

As parents, we would want to do everything in our power to make sure our children felt safe and secure. We never think they have the same worries as an adult, but what if they do?

It is important to talk to your children about their worries and fears, no matter how big or small they may seem. Let them know that it is okay to be afraid of something, and help them come up with a plan to deal with their fear.

If your child is afraid of the dark, try leaving a night light on in their room, or getting them a flashlight to keep by their bed. Help them to understand that there is nothing in the dark that can hurt them, and that they are safe in their room.

Talking to your children about their worries and fears can help them to feel better and more confident.

Children are adults in little bodies, and they have the same worries and fears as we do. So let's not forget to talk to them about their fears.

Some children have a natural fear of the dark. This is perfectly normal and nothing to worry about. However, if your child is excessively afraid of the dark, it might be a sign of an underlying problem. Excessive fear of the dark can be a symptom of anxiety or depression.

There are a few things you can do to help your child cope with their fear of the dark, including:-

- Encourage your child to face their fear by gradually exposing them to darkness. Start with short periods and gradually increase the duration.
- Provide a night light or leave a light on in the hallway so your child can see if they need to get up during the night.
- Reassure your child that you are nearby and will always protect them.

- Encourage your child to use their imagination to create positive stories or images in their mind when they are feeling scared.
- Help your child to understand that their fear is only temporary and will eventually go away.
- If your child's fear of the dark is excessive and causing them distress, it might be worth seeking professional help. A therapist can help your child to understand and manage their anxiety.

Chapter 2: Lucy's Story

This is a story about an amazing child. Lucy was eleven years of age and was afraid of the room she slept in, and also afraid of the dark. She would sometimes wake up screaming in the night.

From an early age, she wouldn't sleep in her bed for long. Every night was the same; she would wake up either in her parent's bed or her brother's bed.

Does that sound familiar?

This had a huge effect on all the family. They looked for help from doctors and counsellors with no answers.

It was so bad they were considering medication.

Would you believe that, medication? Of course, you would, because we are brainwashed to believe that doctors have all the answers. But they are human, just like us. They don't have all the answers, but they do their best.

But I feel that sometimes their best is not good enough, and I do not believe drugs are the answer.

It is your responsibility to find the answers for your children, not the Doctor's, the psychiatrist's, or the counsellor's. But YOURS.

This is her story written in her own words. She is one of the reasons why I am writing this book: to help the children in the world today who are suffering. And to help the parents who have no idea where to get help.

Introduction:

"The lesson I learnt from going to the universe was, don't hold back on how you feel, but don't let how you feel stop you from doing the things you want!

"From a very young age, I was only able to sleep with someone, but never on my own. That scary feeling was just as if someone had a fear of rollercoasters and then went on one. Even when I tried to sleep in my bed I would either stay up the whole night or leave my bed to go to my mum and dad.

"I would be afraid of what was in my room at night, a scared feeling that only I felt, even though nothing was there and my family was under the same roof as me I could never manage to fall asleep. Even when my head was drifting off no matter how tired I was, I would not allow myself to fall asleep.

"I would wake up my mum and dad and make everyone tired, but most of all I was disappointed in myself for not being able to do it. I was so scared but determined, and I tried everything from recordings to books to lavender sprays and more, but none of this stuff, which was meant to work on "everyone", helped.

"So I tried hypnosis, and my parents took me to one of the best people I now know, Geoffrey Loveday."

Session One: The universe

"For the first session, we went to the universe. It started with me walking up a staircase and through a single wooden door. Around me were stars, a pale white light, and the night sky. In the distance, I could see a door appear. I walked up to this door that had just appeared and walked through it. I had walked into another generation.

"People were walking around in dresses and suits. There are old shops, old fashioned cars, possibly from the 1900s. But one woman stood out to me the most.

"She was wearing a long frilly dress with brown boots, She had short brown wavy hair and a few freckles. I looked into the woman's eyes and saw sadness, some sort of fear, the way I would feel at night. I realised we shared the same feelings and that she was one of my ancestors who had passed along to me the feelings that we shared. Although these feelings were not nice and not fair for this woman to keep, I had to give them back to her, they were not mine.

"A dark, black colour left me; the negative energy left me and a white bright light full of good and positive energy fell into my body. A feeling of relaxation and calmness came over me.

"The same happened to the woman who shared the same feelings as me, and when I looked into her eyes she looked happy and free. It wasn't her fault, so I thanked her and waved goodbye before leaving through the door.

"As I came out of the door, stars surrounded me and I was filled with the feeling of being free from all the negative energy. I was ready to leave, I walked through another door, but this time it led to the set of stairs I had originally walked up. Slowly I walked down the stairs, leaving everything behind. As I got to the bottom of the stairs I saw a small gift, I opened it up and found a small gem inside. I took it with me knowing it had positive energy held inside.

"The lesson I learnt from going to the universe was, don't hold back on how you feel, but don't let how you feel stop you from doing the things you want!

"One.. two... three. I was awake and feeling better than usual!"

Session Two: The library

"For the second session, we went to the library. I saw the set of stairs again and had a choice of walking up or down. This time I walked down. Opening the thin wooden door, I saw piles of books and books and books stacked up all over the floor; some old, some new, some beautifully presented, others not.

"But in the centre was a small table, a wooden desk and a chair. I was on my own, with the stars above my head. I sat down looking at a precious golden book sitting in front of me on the table. I opened the book delicately, but as I did the whole library disappeared and I was standing in a disco. It looked like the 1980s, with people wearing colourful clothes and hair up with different types of jewellery. I walked past all these people dancing their hearts out, and in the corner, I spotted a woman sitting alone, with frizzy blonde hair and pale skin with brown eyes.

"I felt as if I also shared a connection with her because when I looked into her eyes I saw sadness and feelings of loneliness, and mixed emotions running through her. Once again these were the same feelings I had before. I knew how it felt, but I had to give these feelings back as they are not mine.

"As before, a dark black colour left my body, the bad energy, and a white light came down, entering me and protecting me from everything. The same thing happened with the woman standing opposite me, with negative energy leaving her and positive energy falling into her. Once again, I looked into her eyes, but this time when I looked she seemed happy, all the opposite feelings of how she had felt beforehand. It wasn't her fault she felt this way, so I waved and smiled at her and left through the door I entered.

"When I arrived back at the library, I sat back down at the brown wooden table and spotted another book. I flicked through the pages, on the first page I turned to it said: "Keep calm everything is fine"

"On the second page, it had a picture of 4 boys all around the same age, with curly hair, some short, some tall. Below the caption read: "Happiness starts with other people"

"On the final page, it read: "You can do it if you put your mind to it," with a picture of a man with curly brown hair and a moustache. He had his thumbs up in the picture.

"All of a sudden the book closed. I stood up from the chair and exited the door once and for all. Walked up the stairs and opened my eyes."

Session Three: The Treasure Map

"For the third session, my last one, I got told to walk up or down the same set of stairs. I chose to walk down them. 1, 2, 3, 4, 5 and I saw the same wooden door standing in front of me. I opened it gently and walked through, sitting down at the table in the centre of the room, where I saw an old piece of paper that appeared to be a treasure map.

"I rolled it out flat, and all of a sudden I was sitting at the same table, but on a beach, palm trees surrounding me and the sky a clear blue above. The sand was white and the sea was a clear bright blue. I stood up, brought the treasure map with me, and walked down a small path until I found the place where the "X" should be. I dug my hands into the sand and pulled out a big golden box. I opened it up and found a red gem and a note reading, "Keep it with you, be safe at all times."

"After I collected this special red gem, I carried on walking along the beach until I spotted a woman with curly blonde hair, old ripped clothes, and a hat perched on her curls. She seemed to share some sort of connection with me, so I walked closer to this woman and sat down beside her on the shore. I looked at her and she looked hopeless, sad, and ready to give up. These were also feelings I had sometimes felt, and though these feelings were not nice and not fair for both of us, I had to give them back.

"As I did I saw the negative energy, a dark shadow, leave my body and a bright white light enter it, replacing the feelings I had before. Knowing that I was safe at all times and only having positive thoughts, the same thing happened to the woman opposite me. A black shadow, the negative energy, left her and bright positive energy entered her body. As I looked at her again, she looked happier and more hopeful.

"Although these feelings were not nice to have, it wasn't her fault, so I stood up to leave. I smiled and waved goodbye wishing the woman luck. Still holding on to the red gem I left, back to the desk and back to the room through the door. I once returned up the stairs, I came out and opened my eyes."

How I feel now.

"The plan was to do six sessions, but with those three it has already worked. When I am in bed, I can now fall asleep without any worry, knowing I am safe at all times. All the stuff I had tried previously; for this to work was a miracle, with the positive energy helping me at night. Just closing my eyes and falling asleep has never felt so good. I never thought I would be able to sleep in my bed again, but hypnotherapy, using inherited therapy, has helped so many people including me.

"Previously when I went to bed I would stay up, get worried and leave halfway through the night. But ever since the sessions, this has not happened again. I only have a positive mind now, which I received from the sessions, making me realise that all these thoughts we have are to do with our ancestors, and how they have passed these feelings down to us. They don't belong to us, so we must give them back.

"I learnt that the only way to do so is with hypnotherapy, with the use of Inherited Therapy and The Loveday Method, which can help so many different people with so many different things. To this day, I have never been so grateful for it and recommend it to anyone struggling with the same things. I now have positive thoughts throughout the day and a healthy mind, thanks to Geoffrey Loveday!"

You have read the story that Lucy has written in her own words and the journey that Lucy went on. Just reading it, it is hard to believe unless you have experienced the journey yourself.

Was it real? Did she really see her ancestors? Did she make it up? And does it really matter?

The only thing that matters now is how Lucy feels.

I hope you are beginning to realise these feelings that we have been holding onto were there before we were born. And the question we need to ask ourselves is…

Are We Reliving Someone Else's Life?

When the conscious mind and the imagination conflict; the imagination always wins.

"No one can make you feel inferior without your consent."

Eleanor Roosevelt

Chapter 3: Bullying

...and how it affects our children in later life.

In the United Kingdom, it is estimated that about one in four children is being bullied. This means that approximately three million children in the UK are affected by bullying. It is also estimated that one out of every four children in the United States is bullied at school.

Bullying can have a profound and lasting impact on a child's mental and physical health, as well as their academic achievement. Therefore we must continue to raise awareness of the issue and work together to find ways to prevent and address it.

Bullying is a serious problem that can have lasting effects on its victims. Children who are bullied often feel isolated, insecure, and helpless. They may experience anxiety, depression, and low self-esteem. In extreme cases, bullying can lead to suicide.

There are many reasons why children bully others. Some children bully because they feel insecure or inferior. Others bully to try to control or dominate others. Still, others do it for fun or because they have been bullied themselves.

Whatever the reason, bullying is never acceptable. If you suspect that your child is being bullied, there are a few things you can do.

First, talk to your child's teacher or school counsellor. They may be able to help identify the problem and put a stop to it. You can also encourage your child to stand up for him or herself and to tell you if he or she is being bullied.

Finally, you can teach your child how to be a friend to someone who is being bullied. By doing these things, you can help your child stand up to bullying and make a difference in the lives of other children.

If you have been bullied, remember that it is not your fault. No one deserves to be bullied, no matter what. You can get help from adults, like your parents or teachers, or from other kids who have been bullied. Just knowing that you are not alone can make a big difference.

If you see someone being bullied, don't stand by and do nothing. Speak up and tell the bully to stop. You could also try to help the person who is being bullied. For example, you could invite him or her to play with you or sit with you at lunch. By taking a stand against bullying, you can make your school and community a safer, more enjoyable place for everyone.

This brings me to my next story...

About ten years ago, I received a phone call from an extremely upset mother. She explained that her daughter was being bullied in school. It got to the point she was so afraid she didn't want to go to school.

I could see how desperate her mother was so I immediately arranged a home visit, not something I usually do, but in this case, I felt they needed my help.

When I arrived the little girl was in the lounge lying on the settee. I noticed that when I was speaking to her she had a nervous twitch.

(Of course, when I am working with a child under the age of 18, a parent must be present at all times.)

After getting to know her and getting to trust me, we set up a plan to help her. Over the sessions, the nervous twitch stopped and the fear that she felt left her. We did six sessions. These were the same techniques I use today. The Loveday Method.

A few months ago I had a new client come to see me. She said she was recommended by a friend of hers. When I asked who it was, she said I treated a young girl of seven around ten years ago, and her name was Sarah.

I couldn't immediately recall who it was because I have worked with thousands of clients since then. She then told me I went to the girl's home, and the penny dropped. I knew straight away who the child was.

I asked how she was, and she gave me a card written by Sarah's mother, explaining that she is now 17 years of age and has grown up to be the most amazing young lady. That she has so much confidence now and has so many friends, and is looking forward to going to university.

The sessions we did completely changed her life. She just wanted to thank me.

Now imagine if Sarah's mother hadn't decided to find another way to help her child, and taken the medical route. What would her life be like now? What do you think would have happened to Sarah? As a parent what would you have done?

"Every great dream begins with a dreamer. Always remember, you have within you the strength, the patience, and the passion to reach for the stars to change the world."
                                                           Harriet Tubman

Chapter 4: Anxiety Disorders in Children

Most children experience some anxiety at certain points in their lives. It is a normal and natural part of development. However, some children may experience more intense or longer-lasting anxiety that can interfere with their daily activities.

If your child is experiencing symptoms of an anxiety disorder, it is important to seek professional help. Treatment for anxiety disorders often includes cognitive-behavioural therapy, medication, or a combination of the two. With proper treatment, most children can learn to manage their anxiety and live healthy, happy lives.

Did you read that? Medication? Manage their anxiety? We don't want to manage it, we want it gone. That's right, gone.

Anxiety disorders are the most common mental health disorders in children. According to the National Institute of Mental Health, an estimated one in eight children aged six to seventeen experiences an anxiety disorder in any given year.

According to a recent survey on anxiety disorders, one in eight children aged five to nineteen had a mental disorder in 2017.[2]

Several different types of anxiety disorders can affect children, including:

1. Separation anxiety disorder – This type of anxiety disorder is characterised by excessive anxiety about separation from loved ones, such as parents or guardians.

2. Generalised anxiety disorder – This type of anxiety disorder is characterised by persistent and excessive worry about a variety of topics, such as school, family, friends, and activities.

3. Social anxiety disorder – This type of anxiety disorder is characterised by extreme shyness or fear of social situations, such as performance anxiety or fear of being judged by others.

---

[2] https://digital.nhs.uk/news/2018/one-in-eight-of-five-to-19-year-olds-had-a-mental-disorder-in-2017-major-new-survey-finds

4. Selective mutism – This type of anxiety disorder is characterised by a child's refusal to speak in certain social situations, such as school or church.

5. Obsessive-compulsive disorder – This type of anxiety disorder is characterised by repetitive thoughts (obsessions) and/or behaviours (compulsions) that the child feels he or she must do to avoid a feared event or situation.

Left untreated, anxiety disorders can have a significant impact on a child's life, causing problems with school, friends, and family. Treatment can help your child feel better and function more normally.

In the long run, the sharpest weapon of all is a kind and gentle spirit.
Anne Frank

Chapter 5: Violence in the Home

…and the effect it has on our children.

Children who witness violence in the home are more likely to experience a variety of problems, including anxiety, depression, aggression, and difficulty forming attachments. Studies have shown that children who grow up in homes where there is violence are more likely to engage in violent behaviour themselves as adults.[3]

There are several explanations for why this might be the case. One is that children who witness violence see it as a normal way of interacting with others and may therefore think it is acceptable to use violence themselves. Another explanation is that children who see violence in the home may learn to associate love and intimacy with aggression and violence. This can lead to problems in future relationships.

This is a story of a young man aged 39. He came to see me suffering from depression, anxiety, panic attacks, fear, and a feeling of being lost. This was just

---

[3] https://www.aacap.org/AACAP/Families_and_Youth/Facts_for_Families/FFF-Guide/Understanding-Violent-Behavior-In-Children-and-Adolescents-055.aspx

the beginning of his story, after we had talked and said he wanted my help when he got home he sent me a text. This is what he had to say.

"Do you think you can help me?"

I rang him straight back and said there are no guarantees, even doctors don't give any guarantees but felt I could help him. He said that he wanted to go ahead. So let us go back in time to see what his life was like as a child.

His mum and dad separated at the age of 4 because his dad was a heroin addict. At a very young age, he saw his mum being beaten by his father with a baseball bat. From an early age, he saw so much violence.

His mum never met anyone else, so life was difficult, and as a child, in school, he never felt he fit in. We don't know what our children go through when they are small and vulnerable, do we? And how it can affect their life as they get older.

Let's go forward in his life from when he first met his wife at the age of 24.

Now, they are married and have two beautiful girls, aged six and three. The amazing thing is, if any of these things that happened at a young age had not, he would have never met his wife and never had his beautiful children because his life would probably have taken him on a different path.

Everything happens for a reason. But what happens now, and can he be helped? Over six weeks, we worked together using The Loveday Method.

Let's see what happened.

Chapter 6: Danny's Story

Session one: The beginning

"I got in contact with Geof as I'd been suffering from severe anxiety and panic. It's been quite limiting, from setting boundaries and comfort zones and not being able to drive long distances, to anticipatory anxiety, sleepless nights and panic attacks.

"My first session was surreal. I really could envision everything from my late relatives who are no longer with us and from being a child going back to when my troubles and fears originated and even settling an old score.

"I'm hoping to be getting back to my confident self and improve my outlook on life without the need for medication."

Session two: The Universe and Hypnotherapy with Geoff

"Today's session was about the universe. It was quite surprising really, using the power of my mind and hypnotherapy moving forward from the first session to making peace with my past.

"Now we looked at my grief and persons I had lost along the journey. I visited late relatives in the universe. It was quite surreal really to be able to pull memories and vivid faces out of my mind.

"I pictured my late grandfather and he gave me a message of hope and strength then colours of all my different chakras entered my body."

"The only person you are destined to become is the person you decide to be."
Ralph Waldo Emerson

There have been plenty of stories of child abuse in families. Unfortunately, this problem still exists today. Child abuse can take many different forms, including physical, emotional, and sexual abuse. It can occur in any family, no matter what their socioeconomic status is.

While it is difficult to estimate the exact number of children who are abused each year, it is clear that this problem is widespread. According to the Centers for Disease Control and Prevention (CDC), approximately one in four girls and one in six boys will be sexually abused before they turn eighteen. Furthermore, it is estimated that one in ten children will be physically abused at some point during their childhood.

What are some warning signs that a child is being abused? There are many warning signs that a child is being abused. Some of these warning signs may include bruises, cuts, or burns that are in the shape of an object or instrument; or frequent absences from school.

Child abuse can have several negative effects on the victim. These effects can be physical, emotional, and mental.

Physical effects can include injuries, such as bruises, cuts, or broken bones. Emotional effects can include depression, anxiety, and post-traumatic stress disorder (PTSD). Mental effects can include problems with memory and concentration. Child abuse can also lead to problems in relationships, such as difficulty trusting people.

If you suspect that a child is being abused, it is important to get help right away. There are several resources available to help victims of child abuse, including hotlines and counselling services. If you are unsure whether or not a child is being abused, trust your instincts and err on the side of caution. It is better to be safe than sorry.

If you are a victim of child abuse, know that you are not alone. There is help available. You can get through this.

Chapter 7: Yvonne's Story

We did six sessions using The Loveday Method, and Yvonne has now found true happiness.

This is a story of a lady who was sexually abused by her grandfather from the age of six to eighteen years of age. Her name is Yvonne, and she is now 39 and has three beautiful children.

I decided to contact Yvonne and ask if she would be willing to write about her life and the unhappiness she felt as a child.

You cannot imagine this young lady's suffering, and now she dared to tell her side of the story.

However, I spoke to Yvonne a few days later and she felt it was too distressing to carry on with the story as it brought back so many bad memories.

I completely understood I did feel guilt for asking her to do this. She is more important than the story…

This is what she sent me after we spoke on the phone.

"Thanks for being so understanding Geoff. Here's how far I got.
You take care and speak to you soon xxxx"

"My earliest memory of my childhood was around seven years of age. I can recall this time when I got a white teddy bear for Christmas and told him all of my secrets. Ted was my only outlet.

"My granddad sexually abused me from around the age of six until I couldn't take it anymore and took an overdose at the age of 18."

Yvonne told me that when she was around ten she was sad, lonely and so afraid, and had no one to turn to for help. She went to a phone box and rang the child helpline, they tried to calm her down, and they said they would send someone.

Would you believe, no one came?

Can you imagine how that child must have felt? Trust me, you can't unless you have been through it yourself.

She has allowed me to finish her story. I am writing to try to feel what she went through as a child, but I can't. It's not my story, it's hers.

Maybe we should look for the good and see where life's journey has taken her. She has 3 beautiful children, she built up her own business, she can trust people again, and she found someone special.

But most of all she has found inner peace and true happiness.

How? Read on and you will find the answers. And where to get the help you desperately need. You are not to blame and it is not your fault.

"We have nothing to fear but fear itself."
Franklin D. Roosevelt

Chapter 8: Nightmares

...and how it affects children.

It's every parent's worst nightmare. Your child is having a nightmare, and you can't do anything to stop it. You watch helplessly as your child thrashes around in their sleep, whimpering and crying out in terror.

It can be tough to know what to do when your child is having a nightmare. You may feel like you need to comfort them and try to wake them up, but that can often make the situation worse. Instead, it's best to let your child ride out the nightmare and offer reassurance when they wake up.

If your child is having nightmares regularly, there may be an underlying cause that needs to be addressed. Talk to your child's doctor or a mental health professional to see if there is any help that can be provided.

Causes of nightmares.

Several things can cause nightmares in children. It's often hard to pinpoint the exact cause, but some common triggers include:

1. Stressful events – A major life event such as a divorce or the death of a loved one can trigger nightmares. Even something like starting a new school or moving to a new house can be stressful enough to cause nightmares.

2. Trauma – A traumatic event such as abuse, a natural disaster, or a car accident can lead to nightmares.

3. Anxiety – Children with anxiety disorders are more likely to experience nightmares.

4. Medications – Certain medications, such as antidepressants and certain allergy medications, can increase the risk of nightmares.

5. Sleep problems – Children who have difficulty sleeping are more likely to have nightmares.

If your child is having nightmares, there are a few things you can do to help them. First, it's important to try to identify any possible triggers and avoid them if possible.

It can also be helpful to establish a regular bedtime routine and make sure your child is getting enough sleep. If anxiety is a trigger, you may need to talk to a mental health professional about ways to help your child manage their anxiety.

It's also important to reassure your child that they are safe and that the nightmare is not real. Let them know that you're there for them and offer comfort if they need it.

If nightmares are a regular problem, you may want to keep a notebook or journal so your child can write down their dreams and nightmares. This can help them to identify patterns and triggers.

Nightmares are often scary for children, but they don't usually cause lasting harm. With some support and reassurance, most children will be able to overcome them. However, if nightmares are causing significant distress or interfering with your child's life, it's important to seek professional help.

Is it possible it was inherited from their parents?

There is some evidence that anxiety, fear, and unhappiness can be inherited from parents to children. Studies have shown that children of parents with anxiety disorders are more likely to develop anxiety disorders themselves.

However, it is important to remember that not all children of anxious parents will develop anxiety disorders. There are many other factors, such as environment and upbringing, which can influence a child's mental health.

There is some evidence that anxiety, fear, and unhappiness can be inherited from parents to children.

There have been several studies conducted on the inheritability of mental health disorders, including anxiety disorders.

One study, published in the American Journal of Psychiatry in 2001, found that children of parents with anxiety disorders were more likely to develop anxiety disorders themselves.

Another study, published in the Journal of the American Academy of Child and Adolescent Psychiatry in 2006, found similar results.

If you are concerned that your child may be at risk of developing an anxiety disorder, it is important to talk to their doctor.

Anxiety Is More Likely to Be Passed From Mother to Daughter.

Although it has long been understood that anxiety tends to run in families, recent studies reveal that anxiety problems are passed down from mothers to their daughters, whereas having an anxiety-free father protects sons.[4]

What are some common causes of anxiety, fear, and unhappiness in children?

---

[4] https://www.sciencealert.com/mothers-more-likely-to-transmit-anxiety-disorders-to-daughters-than-sons

Many different factors can contribute to anxiety, fear, and unhappiness in children. Some common causes include:

- family history of mental health disorders
- exposure to traumatic events
- bullying or other forms of peer victimisation
- poor family functioning or conflict within the family
- having a chronic medical condition or disability
- experiencing poverty or other economic hardship
- witnessing violence or criminal activity
- being a victim of abuse or neglect

There are many different signs and symptoms that can indicate that a child is experiencing anxiety, fear, or unhappiness. Some common signs and symptoms include:

- avoiding activities or situations that make them anxious
- feeling constantly on edge or stressed
- being easily irritable or prone to outbursts
- having trouble sleeping

- experiencing headaches or stomach aches
- acting out in school or having difficulty concentrating
- withdrawing from friends and activities
- exhibiting sudden changes in eating habits

What are some common treatment options for anxiety, fear, and unhappiness in children?

There are many different treatment options available for children who are experiencing anxiety, fear, or unhappiness. Some common treatments include:

- Psychotherapy – This is a type of therapy that can help children understand and manage their emotions.
- Cognitive-behavioural therapy – This is a type of therapy that helps children change the way they think about and respond to situations that make them anxious.
- Medication – In some cases, medication may be prescribed to help children manage their anxiety.

- Relaxation techniques – This can involve things like breathing exercises and visualisation.

Now, it is possible that all these feelings that children are experiencing were there before they were born. And that They Are Reliving Someone Else's Life. It is not their fault and they are not to blame.

Where can you get the help that you desperately need?

Chapter 9: Jenny's Story

A Fear of Spiders

Can you imagine being so afraid at such an early age? This is the story of a lady who was petrified of spiders from the age of two. And as an adult, she still had this same fear.

Her name is Jenny, and this is her story.

"Hi, Geoff,

"I hope you are having a great weekend! I've added to my story and included the journeys we went on and the people I met during our sessions. I hope it is all in order; if there is anything else you want me to add, please let me know."

"Before I saw Geoff, I had been afraid of spiders for as long as I could remember. There was never one traumatic incident that set off my phobia, at least, not one that I can remember. I couldn't look at photographs or drawings or videos of spiders, especially tarantulas.

"I was lucky enough to go to Disney World with my family when I was little, and when we watched "A Bug's Life" 3-D show, I had to keep my eyes closed the entire time the cartoon tarantula appeared. I remember being in grade eight, doing an assignment in biology class about mini beasts, and I was forced to look at a textbook with drawings of spiders.

"Looking at the drawings gave me a headache; I would feel like spiders were crawling all over my skin, and I would be on edge as if the spiders would appear in the room out of nowhere.

"When I was eleven, I visited my cousins in Toronto, and we explored the lake together on a raft. I saw an enormous dock spider at the side of the lake, and I remember being frozen with horror – then I heard my cousins scream behind me, which made me scream uncontrollably too.

"When the adults rescued us, Mike, my cousin's dad, killed the spider with an oar. Mike said that the neighbours across the lake had heard our screaming and had asked him if someone had been murdered – it was years later that I realised he was kidding!

"Now that I have completed Geoff's course, I feel no revulsion or anxiety at all when I look at photographs and videos of spiders. I even wonder why I was afraid in the first place. I understand that spiders cannot hurt me, or even do anything to me, and it's extremely unlikely that I will encounter a dangerous tarantula or spider.

"I am also appreciative of the spiders' environmental impact, and how they get rid of disease-carrying flies. I went to my local zoo recently to see a tarantula and see the tarantula in its burrow and its photograph on the wall gave me no anxiety. I hope to encounter a tarantula up close one day, but until then, I feel confident in my ability to handle a house spider by placing a cup over it and removing it as gently as possible when I am confronted with one.

"During Geoff's hypnotherapy course, I saw myself in a beautiful valley. Although there were spiders there, on the ground and in the trees, I wasn't afraid of them. I saw ancestors whom I'd never met before in our sessions: a woman in mediaeval clothing and a man wearing a loose tunic top and trousers. They were both holding spiders, and Geoff helped me to release their fears as well as mine. In one of our sessions, I went back in time to when I was ten, and I walked along a beach and saw a spider crawl onto the sand. It made me think about how spiders move in a similar way to crabs, and that reduced my fear of them."

What a journey. The change is remarkable. And as Jenny said, "I even wonder why I was afraid in the first place".

Chapter 10: A Journey with Brent

Brent, aged 43, was suffering from depression, anxiety, sadness, unhappiness, and a feeling of abandonment, and was always pushing people away.

Let's have a closer look at Brent's childhood and what he was going through as a child.

Up to the age of seven years of age, there was violence in Brent's home, and he regularly saw his father beat up his mother.

At the age of seven, his mother tried to commit suicide, and he found her lying on the floor. At ten years old, his Mother tried to take her own life again.

What this child must have felt, the unhappiness, fear and sadness he was going through; you cannot imagine what he was feeling.

At age ten his Grandfather, who was his best friend, passed away.

All the things he was going through, I feel are nature's way of strengthening you; but they can make you stronger or weaker.

Brent is now 43. At the age of 31 his cousin, who was like a brother to him was killed in Afghanistan, and at the age of 41, his mother was diagnosed with bowel cancer.

The reason for me to explain my background with Brent is to give you a better understanding of Brent's history and how childhood trauma can have an impact on later life.

Not only can it affect our children, but also the future generations of our children, our grandchildren and great-grandchildren, and as you read on you will begin to realise it was there before he was born.

This is his story.

Session One: The Journey.

"Hi, Geof,

"Thanks for today. Honestly, I don't think I expected anything like that this morning.

"I wouldn't say I was sceptical, that's too harsh a word; more that I didn't think I would be affected, especially in such a way. I've tried to write down what I can remember from the session and again, I apologise, as I'm not the most articulate person.

"When I arrived, you made me feel welcome and relaxed, and once I laid back in the chair with the music and your instructions, I felt totally at peace. Listening to you describe this, as my barriers slowly came down whilst my hands and wrists became weightless, and my hands coming into contact was such a strange sensation; as you say, almost like a magnet was pulling them together.

"Then seeing in my mind both my mum and dad and explaining to them that the sad and angry feelings I have for them are not mine and that I cannot carry on my life with these feelings in me, it was a strange feeling of relief. Then seeing in their eyes that they are happy for me to release this brought a sense of happiness and contentment.

"Taking the stairs.....up to a red door....through into a meadow with a lake and a waterfall to see Ryan and my auntie Beverly was, I'm not going to lie, unbelievable to the point I had to catch my breath. The feeling that they were there, in front of me, both gently smiling as I explained I couldn't hold onto the grief and sadness I felt, needing to live my life and not be afraid, then both of them agreeing that I need to let that go, this amazed me if I'm honest, and it was clear as day.

"The final part where you took me back to childhood was probably the most intense feeling I've ever had as I couldn't get my head around what was happening. And honestly, I'm still trying to understand exactly what happened.

"Watching myself walk for the first time, blowing candles out on my first birthday cake, and even lying on my mum's chest when I was born was nothing short of amazing, but – and this is a big but – when you asked me towards the end of the session if I could see the little boy and did I want to talk to him, when he turned around and it was me, wow!! That blew my mind wide open, standing there, comforting myself and telling the younger me that everything would be ok. Well, I think you saw my reaction well enough.

"I couldn't think of that part too much today as I was breaking down when I did, but it's ingrained in my mind that when the time comes when I feel down, I will call on this, as it was so real and it was so comforting.

"When you asked how long I thought I had been under, I thought "ten minutes, tops", not nearly 90 minutes!

"I hope I've explained myself well enough. I'm looking forward to the rest of the journey."

Session Two: The Universe

"This session was what you said it would be, not as emotional as the first session but still surreal in the way I felt.

"It started again with the stairs and the door but it felt like I was transported out of myself during this as if looking down on myself.

"The part of the session where I saw a man who looked like he was dressed in Victorian clothes with a dark suit on, hat and barrel-chested with a moustache was strange. It was strange to talk to him, and even more so the feelings I felt. At first, I thought I could feel his strength, as that was the aura he gave off, but after speaking to him and being close it was sadness I could feel.

"At that moment I released dark energy, giving back all the negative feelings which I felt were never mine; it was there before I was born. I then began to realise I was holding onto the pain of my ancestors that had been passed down from one generation to the next, and I was living someone else's life.

"I don't believe I've ever met this man before and I have no recollection if I have, but I got the sense when standing in front of him that somehow I had.

"When you brought me back to the room I felt a real sense of calm in my inner self if that makes sense. I can't explain why, but it did, and it gave me a real sense of serenity, which helped given the way work was last week!

"Thanks again Geof, and I'm looking forward to tomorrow."

Session Three: The Library

"My mind is still racing as to what the symbolism of the pocket watch meant but more about that later.

"The session started with you sending me into a deep trance and the part where my hands raised almost of their own will, this still amazes me, as I can sense them moving and twitching but I'm not doing it.

When deep into the trance state, you asked me to describe where I am and I see myself standing in a field, a blue sky above. I have on a T-shirt and shorts and I can feel the grass, soft and lush beneath my feet. I start to walk across the field, with no end in sight but I'm walking anyway.

"It's strange as after a short while a street comes into view. Not a street from now, but more a street from a Victorian or bygone time. I look down and I'm now wearing trousers and a shirt. It's like I have gone back in time to a place and time I've never seen or been to before. I'm walking down the cobbled street to my house, a tired house with not much furnishings, I walk through the front door. I'm waiting for my wife. It's a surreal, surreal feeling.

"After you ask me a few questions, I'm now watching as my wife is in labour, with a neighbour or friend helping her in the bedroom. I can feel my nerves and the sense of being scared for both her and my baby daughter, which is crazy as I have neither! The sense of relief and happiness as both come through fit and well is palpable.

"I then remember you asking me about the door, and going through the door into a library, sitting in a chair and feeling the worn leather of the arms. Opening a book and seeing a memory from childhood of my mum, feeling scared and sad at the same time. I then turn the page and I'm in my grandparent's house in the living room with no one but my granddad.

"I feel scared, as I never really got to speak to him as a young boy before he passed. He was a man's man and didn't have many talks with kids. I tell them both that I can't live their lives anymore and need to let go of the feelings, both my mum and granddad seem happy with this and a sense of relief and contentment comes to me.

"Before I leave the library I find I have a pocket watch; maybe my granddad gave it to me, I'm not sure. But I remember the coldness of the metal in my hand, the solid, heavy feeling of it if that makes sense.

"Maybe this has something to do with my relationship (as brief as it was) with my granddad, but either way, when I came back to the room I felt a sense that I had held this watch.

"I felt calm and content after this session, and I've been thinking of the watch most of the day. Thanks again Geof, as the sessions do leave me with a real sense of calm that I believe I have never tapped into before."

Session Four: The Treasure Map

"Hi Geof, catch up on Tuesday's session.

"The session starts again with you sending me into a deep trance and the part where my hands raised as almost of their own will. This continues to amaze me, as I can sense them moving and twitching, but I'm not doing anything.

"I see myself standing at the top of some stairs, so I go down them to a door, a blue door. You ask me to go through the door and I'm standing in a pasture, trees hugging the perimeter, and I can feel the grass, smell the grass. You ask me to describe this and I do, looking up to see the crystal-clear blue sky.

"I'm wearing shorts, a t-shirt and flip-flops as I start to walk, and you ask me to look for a Treasure Map. I start searching as I'm walking, and then I see it, folded up in front of me, a map.

"I open the map and start to follow the instructions, walking and walking until in the distance I can see somebody. As I get closer I get a strange sensation that it feels like I'm looking at myself. I can't be sure but it feels this way.

"I can sense his anger and this makes me feel apprehensive and nervous. I speak with him telling him I can't take his anger with me and that I need to let it go and live my life. And he seems to be content and happy with me telling him this.

"Before I finish speaking to him ("me" which is crazy, I know) he gives me a gift. It's a small wooden box, which when I open it, has a key inside. I'm not sure what the gift or the key represents, but I understand why I think I was talking to myself. And when you bring me back to the room, I have an overriding sense of relief and calm.

"I felt this calm since Tuesday, and it's helped me so much, given I'm having my six-year-old over the summer holidays and calm is one thing I need to be!

"Thanks again for the session Geof, looking forward to Tuesday and the 5th Session."

Session Five: The Lost Key

"The session starts with you explaining to me about the lost key, although I found this in the previous session, so this is new for both of us. Again it starts with you sending me into a deep trance, with the part where my hands raised as almost of their own will, sending me further under.

"I find myself at a set of stairs; I go down them, leading to a blue door, really deep blue. The door has a lock and with me holding the key in my hand, I try my luck and it fits.

"I walk through the door into a wide open space, a pasture, but not with the blue skies I have experienced previously. The skies are now grey and cloudy. I look around and down at myself. I'm standing on the grass wearing shorts, flip-flops and a t-shirt. I begin to walk.

"Walking and walking I see a person, it feels like I'm looking at myself from a different time, which is a strange sensation.

"But I also sense another person there. I look around and it's like we have gone back in time, I'm dressed in clothes from the turn of the last century. I sense I know the other person. I think it is my great-grandfather Ben, who I never met as he passed away before I was born.

"Weirdly I can sense his pain and hurt and he can feel mine, and sense my building up of walls to protect myself, just as he did.

"I tell the version of myself that I can't take my anger or feelings with me anymore, I need to live my life and let go of these feelings. I then turn to my great-grandfather and tell him the same; these feelings are not mine, they are his, and I need to let them go to allow me to live my life. I sense both of them feel relieved that I have done this and they look happy.

"I feel a sense of relief and calm in myself and when you bring me back to the room I feel this massively.

"Since the session, I'm feeling gradually that each session I am finding myself again and a feeling of inner peace within myself.

"Hope this helps Geof, one more to go!"

Session Six: The Crystal

"Please see my notes from the final session.

"The session starts with you making me comfortable and sending me to sleep, going gradually deeper and deeper until I am under.

"I see a set of stairs leading downwards to a dark blue door. The key I had found in my previous session fits the lock on the door and I unlock it and slowly open it, entering what looks like an industrial unit with huge, wide windows. I can see that the sky outside is quite grey and gloomy.

"I look at what I'm wearing and it's comfortable for me, shorts, a t-shirt and a pair of sliders. As I look back I'm shocked as I now notice that I'm outside rather than in the warehouse, with the sky right above me. Looking up at your request, I'm shocked to see that all of my relatives (both alive and passed) are sort of floating in a calm state. It makes me emotional seeing this, as it's a strange sensation. They are all looking down on me with a look of peace about them.

"You start to bring me back into the room and I can feel the state of calm they were showing has been passed to me. I feel lighter and calmer if that makes sense because as ever, it blows my mind.

"Throughout all of the sessions, I have felt I have been gradually finding a feeling of inner peace within myself and everyone within my circle of family and friends has seen a big change in me.

"I can't thank you enough, Geof, and whilst I hope we don't have to see each other again, I'll miss the sessions a lot, and if I ever take a downturn you will be the first person I contact.

"Kind regards, Brent."

Chapter 11: Jane's Story

When Jane was on a plane she felt trapped and could not breathe there was no way out. But this had nothing to do with a fear of flying. This is Jane's story.

"Sorry, I'm only just getting this over to you now; I have been so busy all day! I'm going to try and explain what happened in our session today as best as I can, so hopefully, you can get something from it!

"Today I had my third hypnosis session. Geoff explained to me that we would be visiting the 'Library of Life' and travelling through time. As always, I was open-minded and ready to see what was coming.

"After putting me into a deep trance (potentially the deepest one I've experienced so far), Geoff asked me to imagine that I was in a room and asked me to explain what was around me. As I looked around, the room was empty. There was a turquoise blue carpet, dark blue painted walls and a white ceiling covered with an Artex pattern.

"Geoff asked me to look down at my legs and to describe who I was. At first, everything was blurry and I couldn't make out who I was at all, but after looking up and back down a few times, the focus started to become clear. As I looked down I could see my camouflage trousers, grey/green steel toe-capped boots with laces and a tight, green t-shirt. I noticed I had a man's body.

"After voicing this, Geoff tapped my head gently and explained I was going to a different place in time to try to gather more information about this man that I had become. As I looked around, I saw I was at the beach. It was a warm, sunny day and I was sitting on the sand and relaxing – still in my army uniform. Ahead of me, two children were chasing each other and playing in their swimsuits.

"The girl was around nine or ten and the boy was around five years old. I sat there just smiling at them. At this point, Geoff asked me to approach the children and speak to them. I did, but they couldn't hear me. They didn't notice me. It was almost like I was invisible. It was at this moment Geoff and I both realised that I had died. I was watching over these children, my children, to watch them grow and keep them safe.

"Once more, Geoff tapped my head and asked me to go back to the moment I had died. Almost instantly I was transported, sitting in a dugout on the ground and still in my uniform. This time though, I had hold of a green bottle of water that was covered in black netting and I was holding it tightly to my chest. There were other soldiers on either side of me and we were all trying to hide, panicking and waiting to be discovered. There was chaos going on above; gunshots, screaming and deafening explosions.

"I could feel the fear so strong inside my body, I had no control over what was happening and I had to just sit there and accept my fate. Suddenly, the noise from above began to get louder and the soldiers all started to run past the dugout. As they ran, piles and piles of mud and soil poured down into the hole I was in and began to bury me. I couldn't breathe, I was being crushed and I was suffocating. Eventually, I was gone.

"I was then taken back to the empty room. I was separated from the man, and I released the negative energy that I'd had all my life into him. It released all his traumas, and then beautiful golden light came down and covered us both. I felt lighter at that moment. I looked at him. A doorway of light surrounded him as he walked through. He looked back at me, thanking me with his eyes as the doorway closed.

"After this, I was guided by Geoff to make my way back to the library and he explained that something had been left there for me to send a message. I looked down and saw the soldier's helmet. I think he was trying to protect me.

"When I had been brought out of the hypnosis, Geoff and I began to discuss what I had seen and the potential meanings behind it. One thing that struck me was the choice of words I always use. If I am ever overly stressed, anxious or facing my worst fear (going on a plane), I always explain that I can't breathe and that I am 'suffocating'. It seems that I have carried this man's death and feelings with me throughout my life and I can feel it.

"Although I am not yet 'cured' and we do still have three sessions to go, I am sincerely overwhelmed with what we have discovered so far. If anything, I am beginning to understand myself more and make sense of why I feel the way I do, and that in itself takes a massive weight off of my shoulders. I somehow feel as though I can breathe more easily.

"Hopefully, that's what you needed Geoff, and thanks again for today!"

Chapter 12: Depression

Depression in children can be hard to spot. The signs and symptoms may be subtle and not always obvious. And children experiencing depression may not have the words to describe how they're feeling.

Still, depression in children is a real and serious condition that can have lasting effects if left untreated.

As a parent, it's important to be aware of the signs and symptoms of childhood depression and to seek help from a mental health professional if you suspect your child may be depressed.

Childhood depression may present itself in different ways than adult depression. For example, depressed children may seem more irritable or cranky than usual rather than sad. They may also exhibit physical changes such as headaches or stomach aches with no apparent cause.

In addition, depressed children may have difficulty concentrating, may sleep too much or too little, and may eat more or less than usual. They may also withdraw from friends and activities they once enjoyed or become more clingy and dependent.

Depression in children can be caused by several factors, including biological factors such as genetics or brain chemistry; psychological factors such as trauma or stress; or environmental factors such as family conflict or bullying.

Childhood depression is treatable. Effective treatments for childhood depression include psychotherapy, medication, and, in some cases, a combination of the two. With treatment, children with depression can get better and return to their usual activities. But it is also possible these feelings that they feel were there before they were born.

There is no one answer to the question of where depression comes from. While some experts believe that certain people may be predisposed to depression due to genetic factors, it is also possible for depression to develop in response to early life experiences or stressful events.

Chapter 13: Tony's Story

Tony was seventeen years of age when I met him, so his sessions always included the presence of a parent. Here, you can see how the traumas of his childhood are affecting him today.

At the age of five, his parents separated, which had a huge impact on Tony's life. He couldn't remember much of his childhood. Repressed emotion is a psychological defence mechanism that occurs when the subconscious prevents you from remembering negative experiences in your life.

For example, suppressed emotions can lead to amnesia from traumas in your early years if you have never dealt with them.

At the age of ten, Tony lost his best friend Harry. At seventeen his Nan passed away. From the age of eleven to fourteen he was mentally abused at school, and his mother took him away from that school.

And during this time he started taking drugs, which affected the family.

I am here to tell you it is not his fault and he is not to blame. Please take the time to read his story, as this is a story of true courage.

The Beginning

"This morning's session with Geoff has changed my life and the way I look at it.

"He played some music and put me into a deep trance. He took me to a place where I felt safe and told me to visualise anyone I have to blame for my pain and suffering. I saw myself, as a younger self who abused his body with drugs to shut out the hurt and hatred that I had for myself. I told him that it was okay and that I am special and loved. This released a burden from me instantly, and the 15-year-old boy who was depressed, confused and couldn't see a way out, smiled and vanished.

"Then, my dad appeared. After getting everything out that has been eating away at me, I told him that it was okay, that everything he put me through was okay, and that I forgave him. I saw the dark black energy leave both my younger self and my father. As it did, I felt the pain leave my chest and I could finally breathe again.

"Geoff took me to the day my dad left, and gave me the strength and confidence to be able to comfort my mum and sister and forgive my dad.

"He then took me to my first birthday. I was there, and my family was there. I remembered every tiny detail; I was reliving a distant memory. It all came flooding back.

"He took me to my birth, and I felt the warmth of my mom's chest and I felt the love that she reflected onto me as soon as she held me. I was truly amazed.

"Due to losing my nana very recently, I wanted to see her. Geof started by letting me picture stairs; they were my nana's stairs.

"With every step, I went deeper into the trance, until I reached the top. A new, shiny, black door presented itself. I took a deep breath and with Geof's guidance, I walked through. I was met with a warm summer morning, on top of a mountain with a beautiful sunrise in the distance. I could feel the grass on my feet and I was at peace. Geof then helped me find the path, a wooden decked path that led me to a lake with a waterfall to my left and endless green fields and the sunrise to my right.

"As I was standing there I saw a light, and out of it came my nana, my granddad and their beloved dog Lucy. I was in shock. There stood in front of me were my granddad who passed away 21 years ago, my nana who I've recently lost, and the family dog from my childhood. They looked alive, happy, well and at peace.

My nana put her hands out to me and I held her and felt an overwhelming sense of relief and warmth. The first thing I said when I lost her was that I needed to feel her hands, and she knew that. I told her that it was okay, and to forgive her for any emotions she has passed down.

"Then to my granddad, I forgave him for anything he passed down to me and told him it was okay. He shook my hand and rested his hand on the shoulder that had carried my nanas coffin. The weight that I had previously felt had been lifted. I felt so much lighter. I gave them both a hug and was then joined by my mum and sister. We were all reunited.

"When it was time to leave, with Lucy the dog by their side, they turned around and walked into the light. Before they did, my nana turned around to me and nodded at me, letting me know it was all going to be okay. It was the most incredible and fulfilling experience I have ever had in my life.

"Geof unlocked the door for me and pulled down the barriers to the place where my nana and granddad could contact me, and see me. This has changed how I feel about her passing, and I am happy she's at rest with my granddad. I have been assured of that now."

Tony is now doing amazing. He is now a qualified lifeguard doing shifts after school, he is learning to drive, is back seeing his dad again, and going to the gym.

I just wanted to let you know that Tony only had two of the six sessions that were scheduled for him. I spoke with Tony's mother. I thought he needed to finish the programme, but they decided he didn't need them right then, since he was doing so well.

That, in my opinion, was a poor choice. It is quite similar to a course of antibiotics.

But only time will tell if I'm right.

Chapter 14: Diane's Story

The Journey.

Diane was 31 when she came to see me. She suffered from depression, anxiety, sadness and panic attacks. She had a fear of being pregnant but wanted a child so desperately. But she could not conceive as she never got over the passing of her father.

She smoked weed from an early age and wanted to stop, but this was a connection she had with her father which had brought them closer when he was alive.

She lost her grandfather at the age of four, her grandmother at the age of nine, and her father, who suffered from depression, at the age of 24.

Her mom's dad died when her mother was 18 years of age and her dad's mum died when he was a young boy.

I feel it is important to know Diane's background and that these feelings and unhappiness she was holding onto were there before she was born and were passed down from one generation to the next. She was living someone else's life.

The First Session

"My first session was everything I hoped it would be. I had hoped for some kind of connection to my subconscious, which is exactly what happened. I had hoped even more for some kind of 'sign' that I was on the right track, that I was doing the right thing. I didn't dare hope for a connection to my dad, who passed away seven years ago, that would have been too big of a wish. But that's exactly what I got, and not in a "medium" type way.

"Geof guided me into hypnosis where I felt safe and comfortable and relaxed. When Geof told me that when he tapped my left hand there would be someone waiting for me and I would know and see them instantly, as soon as he tapped my hand I felt him. My dad's presence was there, which I have been missing since he left this life.

"It's not like we were speaking as we would have done when he was living, but I could feel his love and his smile. My dad was my best friend, but he had suffered on and off throughout his life from depression, which I undoubtedly absorbed as a child. Geof guided me to return to my dad the pain which was his and not mine.

"I returned that pain to him with love and understanding. With empathy, because I know that pain wasn't his either, someone gave it to him.

"Tears streamed down my face continuously, sometimes sobbing as the blocked emotion left my body. The tears were a mix – some sad tears because of how much I had missed him, but mostly happy joyous tears that I was 'seeing' him again, rather than that I was feeling him again. I felt the tears purging all this emotion out of me.

"When I didn't think the experience could get any more emotional or any more transcendent, Geof quietly asked me if there was anyone else there with my Dad. I told him there was but they were small and I couldn't make out who it was. I soon realised it was a child or a baby. There seemed to be a lightness around this child and as I got closer to them I realised it was my child - my future child, not yet born, not yet even conceived.

"Yes, I know – my mind is blown! I have suffered from fertility issues for some years and am booked in to start IVF in the coming months. Since my Dad died, one of the things which made me very sad was the thought that my future children would never know their granddad – what a cool, funny, caring, kind, soft, man he was. It hurt my heart that they would only know him through photographs and stories, that they wouldn't truly feel his love, which is the most powerful love I have ever experienced.

"When I saw my dad with this child, it was as if he was telling me that the baby I will one day be blessed with was with him now, as we speak, waiting for its time to come here, to this life. It's like he was reassuring me that my worst fear was redundant because my future child came from him and was sent by him. As I write this now I can picture one day telling my kid this story when they're old enough to understand.

"Also, every time I have recounted this story so far I've accidentally said 'him' when referring to the baby. I wonder if I'll have a boy. If I do, I had already thought about naming him after his amazing granddad, Edward, but now I definitely will be – whenever his granddad Eddie sends him."

Chapter 15: David's Magical Journey

Let's see what he had to say.

Scene 1 - Entering the Domain

"Walking up the stairs I reach a blindingly white door of pure light. It is flat, with no features and no visible way to open the door.

"I approach the door and though there is no visible mechanism for opening the door, one thought was all it took to open it.

"As the door opens, another world awaits the other side, trees, grass, flowers and stars visible within the bright blue sky. Looking at the world, it looks familiar like I have been here many times before, yet it looks foreign to me.

"I step through and instantly feel the crisp cool air hit my face and raise the hair on my body. While my face feels cool, my body is still warm, I look down and see that I am wearing armour.

"I turn around and I see the door, the portal that allowed me to enter this reality slides closed with no evidence that it was even there, to begin with. Yet I know with just a thought it will be back again."

Scene 2 - The Treasure Map

"Walking through the endless fields of grass, trees and flowers I can see mountains in the background that stretch from horizon to horizon. The sight itself is breath-taking, like an unspoilt picture of nature not yet touched by man.

"As I walk forward, I start to feel something urge me towards a point on the ground, I look down and see a microchip laying on the ground in pristine condition. I pick the microchip up and inspect it before placing it into my armour port.

"My armour sanitises the chip and opens up a holographic map from the projectors on my wrist. The map is of the local area and is full of markings and landmarks. One of the landmarks I recognise and it is the one that pulls me to go towards it.

"Why do I know this landmark? How far away is it? There are no scales on the map. Walking towards the landmark, I start to wonder how long it will take me to get there as I can't see anything on the horizon. As I start to think about the distance, I start feeling a sense of rush as the world around me starts to bend as if to my will.

"I am walking normally but the world around me is moving as if I am travelling at the speed of sound. My vision of the world to the left and right of me begins to blur but looking forward I see a grand house."

Scene 3 - The Lonely House

"As I stop right outside the gates of the house, I can see that the grounds around the house are grand full of pristine grass on either side of the long driveway. The gates open and I walk through onto the driveway with the grand house coming closer into view.

"Approaching the house, I can see the intricate detail of the doorway, the house looking both modern and classic. I feel like I have been here many times before and made lots of memories here with loved ones in the past.

"As I approach the grand double front doors I walk in and am greeted by an enormous hallway that leads to a myriad of rooms and a grand stairway that leads to all the floors of the house. As I walk through each of the rooms, I see a clean and modern house in pristine condition, clean with no mess, not even any dust.

"As I walk through the endless rooms of the house admiring the beauty of the furnishings and the pride that it is my house, something begins to strike me. Where is everyone? My attention suddenly looks around the house for signs of other people but I don't see anyone anywhere. I start to look for pictures, toys, books or clothes but I find nothing except for my things. Am I alone?

"I suddenly feel this odd sensation of sadness yet I am still happy, like the thought of always knowing the path in my life could lead to a lonely outcome. However, this path would be worth it. Was it worth it though?"

Scene 4 - The Twin Flame Shines Bright

"I start to head back out of the house through the front doors and as I walk out towards the driveway again and towards the myriad of cars parked there I suddenly feel a presence approaching me.

"I turn around and see this beautiful elegant woman walking towards me, her eyes glistening in the sun, bright blue and carrying attractive energy. Her walk is strong and powerful, yet elegant and graceful. Upon seeing her I instantly feel a buzz in my heart and a warm sense of love fills me. Who is she?

"As she gets closer I can see that she is dressed incredibly well, with her hair well done and tied up with curls running down the side of her face, her dress clings to her body revealing her well-maintained physique. I look at her face but cannot make out any details only her piercing blue eyes but I can tell that she is a woman that is highly disciplined and looks after her appearance well.

"She reaches for my arm and grabs it; bringing me in closer to her, my heart flutters the instant her energy field touches mine. Who is she? And why does she invoke so much emotion within me? The thought keeps running through my head.

"Suddenly I smell a strong scent of her presence and I am instantly hit with a wave of emotions, of memories, of love. I suddenly remember the vision of my coronation and the woman who is standing behind me in ornate armour. I suddenly realise who she is, she is my Twin Flame.

"Waves of emotion, power, strength, faith and vision fill my entire body as if all my memories have become complete. No, as if all my soul has just become complete. It feels as if I've become another person with her around me. I feel incredible, I feel like a king."

Scene 5 - The Regret and The Release

"However, even with the waves of emotions coursing through my body I still feel a massive loss of the kids I have had throughout my lifetime. Was this the only way?

"My mind says yes, but my heart says no. In my vision there is conflict. I know in my vision there is a moment when all of us stood together before my coronation and I felt so complete in my life. This reality didn't match that vision. I deserve more.

"I pull myself, my essence away from the body I am in and I turn around to look at the avatar that I have inhabited. I realise that my avatar is older, maybe mid-40s. I realise that this is just one of many alternate realities that have played out but this is not for me.

"I hold my avatar's shoulder and look him in the eyes, he stares at me knowing exactly who I am. I tell him "this life is yours and not mine; this is not fair on me nor you. I release all this reality back to you."

"A purple cloud leaves my body and travels back into him, then after a few seconds, as I am speaking the words to him, it starts to leave him and climb up towards a cloud of white light above us. The white light covers us both, cleansing us both of the negative energies and releasing us from the grip of the alternate world.

"I feel a sense of relief and oneness. I see his face for the last time, full of smiles as he turns back to his twin flame. I feel a sense of pride, happiness and excitement for my chance to find my twin flame."

Scene 6 - The Return

"My vision starts to fade and I exit the compounds of the house. My world starts to blur as I return to the place I first entered into this reality.

"The blinding white door opens, showing me the path back to my reality. Before I take it though, the map on my wrist makes a noise and starts to float off my wrist and back onto the ground upon where I first found it. Its job is now done, it goes back to rest.

"I make my way through the door and just before I do, I turn around and view this world for the last time, happy that in this reality, whilst I am missing my girls, at least I have found my twin flame.

"I walk through the doorway and it closes behind me to seal another alternate reality which is not mine, forever."

Chapter 16: Amy's Story

Amy came to me when she was 31 years old looking for help with weight loss and emotional trauma.

Session One

"I decided to visit Geof through a family recommendation. Hypnosis isn't something I had ever thought of before, or understood could help with my issues. What I wanted from my session was to feel happy and let go of this weight I feel on my shoulders all of the time. I want to achieve weight loss, but I feel that I needed to deal with the emotional baggage that I have kept for so long before I could even think about attempting to sort my weight out, and I figure the two go hand in hand as I have been comfort-eating my way through life, or either overindulging or not eating at all, and it has always come from a place of instability with my emotions.

"I entered my first session not knowing what to expect, and felt anxious, yet excited, and a little scared about what was to come. I knew from our previous chat that this session would involve going back to some sad moments in life and potentially meeting people who had caused sadness but also experiencing true joy and love. I was ready for whatever was to come.

"After my session started, Geof took me back to a moment in my life from childhood which I had completely blocked out from my mind, and which I now know was my 'suppressed emotion'. I wasn't expecting the wave of emotion that came with it, and I was suddenly a five-year-old little girl again, terrified and afraid.

"I was taken back to a time when my grandfather was abusive to me, my grandmother, and my sister and relived those emotions which I had buried so deep. Geoff was able to help me relive that moment over and over again, each time enabling me to feel a little stronger, less afraid, and more in control, until eventually that moment in my life suddenly felt easy to get through. I don't know how he did it but I suddenly felt ok, calm.

"That moment in my life, I feel, was the start of many traumatic moments that came after. And although it was painful to go back and experience that again, it was also amazing to be able to assure my younger self that it will be ok and that whatever pain was to come would be ok because I, (my older self) would be there to guide and protect the younger child. I hugged myself and assured myself things would work out.

"We then moved on to dealing with speaking to those people who had hurt me in life, and the raw emotion that came with that was hard, but at the same time, it allowed me to let it out and let it go. To finally have them sit there, listen to the damage that had been done and pass that hurt back to them for them to release. It was breath-taking to live through that and be able to have my say and not suppress anything anymore.

"It is mind-blowing how this all took place and these people appeared in front of me as though it was happening in the present. The feelings I had of letting those dark emotions go and receiving the beautiful energy that I should have had all along, was truly a blessing. I could feel a weight lifting and I forgave those that hurt me, and in doing so, let go of any hurt I held. Geoff was just amazing at guiding me through that.

"We also went back to when I had taken my first steps as a child, which was remarkable. I could feel the determination, and lack of balance (which was a strange feeling), but also how proud my Mum was watching me, clapping for me.

"We also went back to the day I was born, which was a surreal experience, looking at my mother through my new-born eyes. I could feel the love that was there, which was beautiful. We also then went back to when I was in my mother's womb and the strangest feeling of almost floating.

"I could feel what my mother felt at that moment, a mixture of worry, anxiety, and sadness, which we got rid of, to feel the joy and happiness that came after. I have never felt anything like it before.

"We then moved on to the spirit world, where I got to meet my loved ones again. One thing that struck me was when I entered the spirit world through the door, my daughter was with me, I was very aware of her presence there, holding my hand. I got to introduce her to my grandmother, my uncle, and my great-grandmother and also got to have many cuddles with my childhood dog, Cindy.

"One of the main feelings I struggle with is feeling alone, and I got to hear from my loved ones that I am not alone; they are always with me.

"This was a gift I could never repay to Geof, who guided me through this rollercoaster of emotion. I got to feel my Grandmother's hands again, I can still smell the scent of my dog Cindy and it was truly amazing to be there in that moment again and feel the overwhelming love from them all.

"After my first session, I came home and cried. I don't know why, but I felt I had to let it out, and I did. I feel a sense of relief that I am letting go of this energy I have stored for so long, which has served me no purpose other than making me sad and depressed. I feel lighter, brighter and ready for what is next to come.

"One thing I did click on after I left my session was that when I first met Geof for our first initial chat about my issues, we did go to a set of stairs when I was hypnotised, and I remember telling Geof that I was scared when I was there, and I told him I was five years old. When we went back to a time when I was most afraid today, I was again, a five-year-old little girl.

"This wasn't a coincidence and only now do I understand why I was initially afraid when I first came to those steps and realised I was a scared five-year-old.

"Being in Geof's presence is a gift. He is remarkable at what he does, and this is coming from someone who didn't know what to expect. From the second I met Geof, I felt calm and comfortable, and his energy was captivating. He is a genius at what he does and such a calming presence to be around.

"I am looking forward to what is next to come in our next session because what I have experienced so far is breath-taking. I am ready to be happy."

Did you read that? Isn't that what we all want, to be happy?

Session Two

"Firstly, I want to explain how I have felt the past week since my first session. I have woken up each day with more energy, more determination and a feeling of purpose. I have attended the gym 4 times this week and pushed past things which usually would fill me with anxiety.

"An example is asking a complete stranger for help with equipment at the gym, never in my life did I think I would be confident enough to approach someone for help in a gym setting, but I did this week. I am also feeling happier and more content and finding it easier to go to sleep at night.

"Having explained the above, I felt excited to attend my second session. We started the session briefly discussing what was about to happen (Geoff didn't mention how absolutely amazed I would be at what was to come though! Wow). As I entered the trance-like state, I walked up the stairs into the abyss. It's truly magical experiencing this and feeling every emotion that comes with it. I went to a place where I met an ancestor.

"I must admit I had no clue what to expect with this because it seems unimaginable that you can go to a place where this can happen but honestly, it happened. The lady (I want to call her Mary) was dressed in what I can only explain as a Victorian-style long dress and dark, worn shoes. Geoff asked me what era she was from and I recall mentioning the 1800's which would fit how she was dressed, she almost looked like a maid. I felt an overwhelming sadness and loneliness from this lady that mirrored how I have felt recently.

"It was almost like we were one. I didn't feel afraid though, the feeling I got from her wasn't evil or bad-natured, just a deeply saddened woman. We held hands whilst I passed her the dark energy back and she released it back to the universe and we were filled with light. She thanked me almost like she had been waiting for this, to be freed. She kissed my cheek as she left and wished me well; a truly remarkable feeling.

"As I left, I was greeted by a small child-like energy. This little lady held my hand, I couldn't see her but knew and felt her presence there. I assumed and mentioned to Geoff that it was my daughter, Grace, but as we moved on I had an overwhelming feeling that this wasn't Grace, it was me. I can see why I thought this little girl was my daughter because we are alike in energy but I know that this little girl was little Amy.

"We hugged, taking in the energy of the stars and feeling every parcel of loving energy that came our way. I found this magical but also, as Geoff guided me through the Universe, he mentioned that I would receive the love and light from the stars, but in my trance, I was already receiving this before Geoff mentioned it, almost as though the Universe knew what was coming and guided me there anyway.

"As I came back down to Earth, I entered an island. I can picture this island so clearly, there was crystal clear water, a cloudy blue sky and golden sand. My little spirit was still there holding my hand as we turned and walked up a cobbled path which led us to the most beautiful meadow-like field. It was filled with flowers, grass and water. It was now time to receive the chakra energy into my soul and we carried on walking through this path.

"With every step I took I received a different energy, starting with the brightest red energy which changed everything around me to the most beautiful red colour. I could feel this energy in me accepting what was being gifted. We then moved on to the other chakra each time receiving and feeling the energy each chakra brought to me until I met a beautiful rainbow, which contained all the chakra colours.

"At the end of this rainbow, there was an envelope addressed to me. As I opened it the message read "It wasn't your fault". I didn't view this as something for me to believe, I already accept things in my past haven't been my fault, this was more of a closure message. I also received a note stating "forgive yourself", which I do, finally. Things happen in life sometimes out of your control and if you are consumed with guilt, sadness and torture, you will never move onto better things. These messages I received didn't make me feel sad; I felt happy acknowledging them and releasing them. I had closure.

"I felt content leaving the rainbow and heading back down the path where I arrived at the crystal clear waters again, this time, the sky was clear too. Not a cloud in sight. I looked into the water and the reflection staring back at me was a happy and healthy Amy, a much slimmer version of having shed the weight of the world. The version I will be. I then left the island not looking back and entered the room where I was met with the steps back to reality. As I was walking back down the steps I envisaged myself shedding a skin (almost like a snake shedding its skin) and with each step I took another layer came off until I was finally at the last step and it was all gone. Before

I knew it I was back in the room with the most amazing weightless feeling as though I had just let go of so much I was holding on to.

"I will be honest; I was sceptical going into this appointment, yes. I had no idea how I could go and meet an ancestor but it genuinely happened and it shocked me. I have no knowledge really of Victorian times or the 1800s as I am not clued up on history so the fact I mentioned that my ancestor was dressed like a Victorian lady etc blows my mind. It was only by looking up what a Victorian lady's dress looked like after leaving my appointment that it made sense.

"Geoff again is incredible, and I am so lucky my path led me to meet him. I believe everything happens for a reason, and I am glad that my journey led me to Geoff and this incredible experience. I feel the benefits of these appointments already and am so excited for the next one."

Session Three

"I have been feeling ok since my last session which was 2 weeks ago. There have been bouts of anxiety and a general feeling of low motivation which was discussed with Geoff and Geoff explained these feelings can be normal given that we are going through highly emotional sessions at times. Reading

Geoff's book in between sessions ``Are you reliving Someone Else's Life?" has helped me and gave me a feeling of 'I am not alone also which was comforting. Sometimes it is so easy to believe you are all alone in what you are struggling with but the reality is, so many people out there are struggling also and we are all in this together.

"We began the session and as always, a sense of immense calm as I was being hypnotised. I approach the door which this time appeared completely different, almost marble-like and very 'fancy'. There were clear numbers on this door as well which is different to previous sessions. As I entered the door, I was suddenly in a field, I could see a house ahead in the distance (I had the feeling I was in America).

"I entered this house which was old and wooden with chipped paint and as I looked around, I could see a room with a rocking chair. I sat in the rocking chair and before I knew it, I was in another house. I could see a small child with red hair and soiled clothing sitting at the dinner table. There was an older lady figure cooking on the stove what appeared to be rice pudding. The family looked starving and I could feel worried and upset about the Mother.

"There wasn't a father figure there or at least I didn't feel one, but there was the eldest Son who even though young, took on the role of the protector of the family, wanting to look after his little Sister. Only now coming away from the appointment I realise that he is relevant as I have had these emotions toward my Sister my entire life. Always wanting to protect her and look after her, shielding her from issues we have had growing up. These feelings are not mine anymore, they are his and have been passed back to him. I didn't realise the relevance at the time but can see it now.

"Moving on to the little girl, I have struggled with weight my entire life, the little girl was clearly starving and I have always had a sense of worrying I won't be full or worrying I won't have another meal. I have never fully understood this desire for food or to overeat but it was clear from seeing this little girl, they are her feelings, not mine.

"The Mother was also worried about feeding the kids, money was sparse and her priority was feeding her children. Geoff asked me what occupation the Mother had and I got a feeling she was working in cobblers for not much money at all. Her feelings of worry about money also mirror mine; I constantly worry about money and the lack of it. I now understand they are her feelings, not mine. I did release those anxious feelings back to her but only now do I understand what they represent. They are her feelings and not mine to hold.

"I passed back the dark energy to the Mother, little girl and Brother and told them "these feelings are yours not mine". I felt a sense of freedom and relief when this happened. It just made sense! The family left and thanked me for freeing them and I also felt thankful to pass back that energy that served me no purpose and release it.

"After the session, Geoff and I discussed this encounter and I believe the little girl had something to do with chimney sweeping. Her face was covered in soot and her clothes were dirty and worn. We also discussed this little girl and Geoff mentioned he wished he would have taken me to her death, to try to understand her life a little more and it suddenly came to me I had an overwhelming gut feeling she had passed during childbirth.

"This also mirrors my life in that I had a traumatic childbirth myself where my Daughter was injured and I nearly lost my life. These feelings I suppress but I understand now they are her feelings and I have passed them back. The similarities between that family and me are mind-blowing and even now, I am amazed at how their feelings have been passed down to me.

"I then entered another field after leaving the home, I could see another old-style home and I entered the home feeling a little anxious. I could see a library-style room to the left of the front door, the same room I have seen previously. In this room, there was a lit fireplace and a wall of books with a rocking chair in front. I sat in the chair and a red book appeared.

"When this book opened, a picture of my father became clear. I entered the book and that memory, because it is a memory for me, I was taken back to an early morning in my childhood when I was 6/7 and I was on the running track with my dad. He was making me run until I felt physically sick. This makes sense to me where my fear of exercise has come from. I always feel anxious about exercising and how uncomfortable I would feel doing it.

"The reality is that exercise is good and releases endorphins which make me feel great. I have never left a workout in my adult years feeling bad! Those feelings I had as a child though came rushing back and I felt uncomfortable and uneasy. I was exhausted and I felt physically sick. I released that dark energy back to my father and told him this was not mine to have.... nor was it his! We released it from him also.

"On reflection, I think these emotions for my Dad came from competitive running with his brother and he always felt second best. My Uncle committed suicide in his twenties and I feel like my Dad then carried on this excessive exercise and put those pressures on me, which I now see wasn't fair. It wasn't his fault though and I can see clearly that releasing this energy for us both needed to happen and I can see where this came from now.

"Understanding the origin of the problem helps in making sure that those suppressed feelings can be understood and therefore released. I hope that my attitude toward exercise changes because deep down I know the benefits of it, I just had this uneasy feeling whenever it came about. Time will tell how my mind changes toward this.

"I was then taken to another memory from the book, this time I was 19 and it was my Mother. She was shaming me for "eating her out of house and home" when the reality was I paid for my food, I was working and I only ever ate what I bought. The shame I felt though, from that comment added to the embarrassment I was already feeling about food and exercise and looking back, this was around the time I started putting weight on.

"I always have a sense of embarrassment when I eat in front of anyone. I feel like people are looking at me and thinking about how overweight I am. I understand these are not my emotions to have! I released this back to her as well and we let it go and I forgave her. They are not my feelings to hold on to and I felt a sense of peace once I had let them go.

I was then back in my rocking chair with the red book. This time the journey took an unexpected turn when I was given a gift from the book which came from my Guardian Angel who I know is my Nan. I was given the locket that she gave me for my 18th birthday after she had passed away. This was a reminder to keep this locket with me to protect me and guide me. My Nan told me I needed to stop punishing myself all the time, "it is doing you no good!" she said in a concerned voice.

"She reminded me of all the good I have in my life and showed me clearly a picture of my Husband and Daughter and showed me this is the good life I wanted and that I have it so to stop letting these past emotions hinder my future. I then lay down on the grass which was softer than anything I have ever felt and my Guardian Angel released the negative feelings I have and replaced them with unconditional love. A feeling of total weightlessness. Just like that, she was gone, I didn't feel sad though, almost like I know she is there no matter what and that comforts me.

"It was now time to leave but what struck me is as I approached the doorway to come back, I still had the locket in my hand. I was bringing this back with me to protect me. I came home and found my locket from my Nan and I am now keeping this with me at all times.

"I am going to try and set a routine for myself this week, going to sleep at the same time each night and waking up at the same time each morning. Trying to fit 4 gym workouts in and taking things one step at a time. These are feelings I had after leaving the appointment which I feel has been given to me as an instruction from my Higher Self, almost like she is saying "This will help".

"I am looking forward to my next appointment to see where this wild journey will take me next."

Session Four

"I have been feeling a lot better and more focused since my last session. Almost like a fog has cleared and I now feel like I'm on the path I am meant to be on.

"We started our session discussing my diet and Geoff gave me guides on how we can improve this which will help clear my mind etc. We then discussed how I'm feeling and we focused on my anxiety. We started the hypnosis by working on the energy related to my anxiety and I could feel it in the pit of my stomach, almost like a fireball.

"Geoff guided me and we focused this energy on my left arm. My arm raised into the air and then Geoff asked me to rest my arm again, this time, when I was about to raise my arm, Geoff said that 50% of my anxiety had gone and left my body so when I next raise my arm it won't raise fully and will only raise 50% of the way. I then raised my arm and it literally couldn't go any higher than 50% of the way, Geoff explained that the negative anxious energy had left and I looked at my hand and realised it had!

"We then repeated this until all of that anxious energy had left. The feeling was unreal and I can't quite put into words how it felt but it was surreal. I could feel the energy shifting from one body part to another and we released the negative toxic energy as we did I felt it leave and that fireball I had in my stomach was gone, absolutely amazing!

"Geoff then guided me to a set of stairs, this time the stairs were concrete painted red with white stripes on either side (they reminded me of school!). There wasn't a door at the top but rather a large window with very bright white light shining through which I could feel the energy from. I was guided up the stairs and as I entered the light, I was suddenly taken to a cobbled street. I had a feeling it was the 1600's but I couldn't be sure. It was olden times.

"Geoff asked me who I was and what was happening if I could see anyone. I knew I was a young boy, "Jack" was his name. As I looked around I could see an older lady (older than Jack, maybe in her 30's) and she was waving her hand beckoning me over to her. Geoff asked what I felt when I saw her and I felt a fire-like energy but not in the sense of danger, it was more like a fire energy which I felt was her pain and anguish. She was loving, and I felt like she was Jack's mother or a mother-like figure to him.

"We entered an old house which then turned into a bakery. I had the feeling we lived there and Jack's mother worked there selling bread. I was then guided downstairs which were the living quarters of the building and suddenly Jack was in bed, he wasn't well and he was suffering. I had an intense feeling in my stomach almost like there was an ulcer, it was painful and Jack was struggling with it.

"As this happened I could feel my stomach hurting and it was gurgling. Jack was hungry, but couldn't eat, possibly due to the ulcer. He hadn't eaten in 3 days. I felt he was dying and I feel like it was food related. He had eaten something rotten and it led to stomach issues which later killed him. His mother was overcome with grief and didn't know how to help, I feel like she didn't know what was wrong with him.

"I was there with Jack in his last moments and as he passed away, he was met by his grandmother (who I felt was a relation to my grandmother) he passed peacefully and as he entered a bright white light with his grandmother, my stomach pains also left. Almost like the route of the problem had been settled. I passed back Jack's problems to him and said it was his and not mine and we released it from us both. It was now time for me to leave.

"I entered the white light again and before I knew it I was awake. This was the most intense session I have had in that I could feel everything so clearly. I could feel my stomach pains, I could feel the anxiety leave me, I could feel it all. Also, the scenes I was experiencing were so vivid and I could see everything so, so clearly! I feel like something left me yesterday after the session, in the best way possible.

"Since the first session, I have felt personal growth for myself so much. 5 weeks ago, my instinct would be to run from anything that made me feel uncomfortable, whereas now, although those uncomfortable feelings are still there, I can push past them a lot more easily, the anxiety isn't holding me back.

"I have also noticed I have a waist! My waist seems to be shrinking inward! I have had compliments about my weight loss from colleagues and family and most importantly I notice it myself. I'm not consumed with thoughts of food all the time, I am seeing food now as nutrition for my body and not always thinking of the next meal! I am fitter myself also and I feel happy! We have a couple more sessions to go and I won't sit and say it's been all roses and sunshine. After some sessions, I have felt down, but only for a few days as those feelings leave my body (they have to go somewhere!) and each week I feel stronger and almost like my body is resetting itself.

"Geoff genuinely cares, the people he helps he does from a place of love. Thanks for everything this far Geoff, I am looking forward to the next session."

I hope you can see the change in Amy, as the layers are taken away.

Session Five

"The fifth session was the Lost Key. We started the session with the staircase which led to a door which was glowing with light. Around the door, I noticed a key was peeking out of the door mat in front of the door and the key was huge, it was a big, thin golden key.

"As we unlocked the door I entered a room which looked like what was my Nan's living room. I was a child, 7 years old, but I didn't feel like me, I felt like I was in young Amy's body but I had a different personality, full of energy and aiming to please. I had my running shoes on and was eager to get going. It wasn't something I wanted to do though, I felt like I was being pushed to do this but the reason I was happy is that I was fulfilling someone else's desires.

"There is a history of running in my family, my Father and Uncle used to go running all the time and I feel like this moment that I felt was part of that.

"I was forced to go running as a kid and always felt not good enough, or that I wasn't doing enough and I think this is maybe why I was taken back to this. I feel like it has come from my Father and Uncle and the way they felt about it. I passed the dark energy back to the child and we released it to the universe. All of that pressure was gone. I then left the living room and a vortex-like glow appeared I entered it and was suddenly in a tunnel. The tunnel was long but I knew where we were going before I even got to the end of the tunnel.

"We were at my Uncle's grave. My Uncle died when I was only 2 years old but I have a connection with him that is unbreakable. I still feel like I knew him inside and out, a lot of similarities in my personality-wise.

"As I was looking around I was standing in front of his grave, I was 13 years old (the same age I was when I found out about how he passed away), and I could see everything crystal clear, the trees, the sky, the flowers. Behind the grave stood my uncle, smiling at me. I started crying and we hugged so tight. He said he was sorry for how he left us. (My Uncle committed suicide at a young age and it was something that then led to issues with my Father, depression in the family and a hole that has never been filled for everyone.)

"I told him it was ok and I missed him. I told him I didn't want to leave him, and I wasn't ready for him to go but he said it is ok, I am on the right path and it will be fine. We hugged so tight I could feel it. That was a hug I have needed for the last 29 years. He gave me the strength to carry on and move forward, and I know he is proud of me. I also gave him back the negative energy I have been carrying and we released it both from him and me. He left and I said my goodbyes, probably for the last time.

"I took a short walk around the grave and walked up the stairs to leave and there was a giant vortex light again with a door and I entered it and closed the door behind me, locking it as I left. I was then met by an old wooden chair, I sat on the chair and suddenly about 50 or so angels were flying around me. They were lit up golden and had the warmest beautiful energy about them. If you can think of Tinkerbell from Peter Pan, that is what they looked like.

"They flew all around me, giving me tiny little kisses as they passed. Each kiss was like a little piece of love they were giving back to me to build me back up. I felt a warm fuzzy glow all around me inside and out as though the hole I felt in my stomach was being filled again. Now it was time to leave and I walked out of the door, locking it behind me and walked down the stairs.

"What I have taken from this session was that there was clearly a void left when my uncle passed and I have never fully gotten over it. I used to train with my Father and I didn't particularly like running but I felt like I had to. I felt like I had to fill this void for my Father because his running buddy was no longer there and somehow it was my responsibility to replace that, but it can never be replaced, he can't be replaced and it wasn't my job to do that.

"I have felt intense pressure my entire life about my weight, and exercise and it got to the point where I had this excessive negative energy around the whole thing. It isn't a healthy attitude but I feel like I am fully understanding where this has come from and in doing that I can close the door on that and move forward. I am 30 pounds down in weight since the start of the year and I am making every step to continue this loss and make healthier changes to create better habits. Not letting this negative mind set I have had for so long get in the way.

"Geoff has helped me understand things so much better and clearer and I don't think I would have gotten to the place I am now without him. I look back on how I felt 5 sessions ago and I am a different person. I am so much happier and that is what will get me to my goal weight. The happiness needed to come first before the weight could leave."

Session Six

"Our sixth session started with a set of stairs, this time the stairs were black, metal stairs which led to a door at the top which was glowing with light. As I entered I was taken to a garden, the grass was green and the sky so blue. As I looked around I noticed a huge tree to my right and at the base of the tree, there was a pink crystal. It looked like a large rose quartz crystal and it was glowing. I picked it up and felt the energy from it in my hands.

"As I looked to the sky, holding the crystal, I could see hundreds of my ancestors in the sky, all lined together staring back at me but one stood out and it was my paternal Grandmother who had passed. She looked just like she used to, in her cardigan and long skirt. Her smile is still as glowing as I remember it.

"Before I knew it we were going back to my grandmother's life events and I was taken to an orphanage when she was a small child. The energy I immediately felt was horrible and I didn't feel like myself at all, the energy around this place was awful and painful and I could feel it all. The stress of this caused my Grandmother to lose all her hair and develop alopecia when she was a child and her hair never recovered or came back. I was told she had long beautiful auburn hair when she was a child and I could see this in my vision.

"All of the children in the home felt similar and were scared and lonely. I gave this energy back to my grandmother and we then released this pain from her also. It does not serve either of us and we released it and replaced it with golden, beautiful energy instead.

"We then went when my Grandmother was older, she was birthing twin boys but sadly she lost both of them. The pain again that I felt was awful, it was a pain that can't be explained properly, like a burning in my body but worse. We again released this dark energy back to my Grandmother and in turn released this from her. The weight lifted felt such a relief.

"My Grandmother had such a painful life but she always had a smile on her face. To feel some of the pain she felt was heartbreaking but I know I have been carrying this with me which has led to issues in my life. She had diabetes and was overweight and I feel that myself.

"I often get told I look like her. It is almost like all these sessions have led to this moment which needed to happen and I needed to get to this point to be able to move forward. As my Grandmother left, she smiled and told me it would be ok and I was on the right path and she left. It wasn't a hard goodbye though, it felt right.

"I then left through a glowing door and closed it and locked it as I left. I was then in another world, a world where I was me but also I wasn't, like another dimension almost. I could see a large factory and everything looked gloomy! I saw a large red, metal door and I entered this door leading me to a work hall.

"Everyone was on machinery and it was the year 2800 (or thereabout) everything was advanced but all of the workers were miserable, it was like everyone's free will and life had been removed from them.

"The only thing around was work and there was no hope or joy in anyone's life. Everything was run by a higher government and there was an overwhelming sense of pain from all. That feeling of no hope was so hard to feel, without hope what is left? I could see everyone was rationed food and again here I am in a situation where I am hungry. I looked around and everyone wore the same clothes, a beige uniform and everyone looked the same. No one had the freedom to express themselves and everything was controlled.

"The more I look at this situation the more I see similarities in how I have felt. I work so hard, and I never stop but at times I feel like it controls me. That leads to stress and that makes me overeat for comfort.

"This is something that has eased over the last few weeks because through the sessions I have learned to release what doesn't serve me but I could see why I have been taken to this place and the message for me was clear. The message was gratitude. Seeing what someone's life is like without hope was awful and it has reminded me that no matter what, even problems can bring you to a better place.

"I will be honest, I couldn't wait to leave and I gave this energy back to this girl (who was me, but also wasn't, I have no other way to explain that ha ha) and we released it. I never want to feel what she feels again and as I left, I locked the door behind me and pulled the shutters down on that door so nothing could get through. I then entered another room, like a hallway and entered another door which I also shut behind me and pulled the shutters down. There was no chance anything was getting through. Before I knew it I was back in the room and felt different, in such a good way!

"I will be honest, I didn't know what to expect at all when first meeting Geof, part of me was telling myself I didn't need this, I could push through but I have been pushing through my entire life and at some point, you need to deal with what is inside rather than running from it.

"I am a different person now, in such a short space of time. I feel like I have let go of so many things, things I didn't even realise I was holding on to. I feel lighter, I am 2 dress sizes down! I am sleeping better. I am getting through the day without a heavy heart and for sure I can say I am happy. I am grateful for everything I have, the good and the bad. I believe everything happens for a reason and I met Geof because I was meant to, this part of my life was meant to happen and I am now ready to move forward and live freely without all this pain I have been carrying with me.

"We have mentioned we will monitor my situation over the next 12 months, see how I get on and if there are any other issues that arise we will deal with them but I am thankful to Geof for helping me and guiding me and bringing me to a place where I am comfortable in my skin. I am excited to move forward now and not look back."

I hope you're starting to see that the feelings we're holding on to have been there since before we were born. And that we are not to blame, it is not our fault. And we are repeating the emotions and feelings of our ancestors. Remember one thing; life is a continuation of the life before.

"The power of imagination makes us infinite."

John Muir

Chapter 17: Jerry's Story

"I found Geof after trying many different things over the years to help me with anxiety and the accompanying coping mechanisms of comfort eating and binge drinking. I have secretly struggled with anxiety issues, including social anxiety and OCD-type thoughts since I was a child but I would say they developed following the sudden death of my mum when I was 14. Up until then, I would say I had a mixed childhood, with some good and plenty of bad memories so that by the time I reached my teens I had a pretty low opinion of myself. I had also begun to develop a bad habit of avoiding situations I found uncomfortable which fed my social anxiety.

"Like most in my circle, I discovered booze in my early teens and instantly loved the way it let me forget my stifling inhibitions and express myself. Coming from something of a boozy family, I found myself mates with the heaviest drinkers whose main goal was getting wasted. I'd often end up overdoing it, acting out of character and due to the trauma of suddenly losing my mum, getting upset during a heavy session. This would be followed the next day by terrible, crippling anxiety and embarrassment. My troubled mind would often blow it out of all proportion and needing comfort, I would turn to food to try and plug the deep sadness I felt inside.

"Things have been a lot better since those dark teenage years when I couldn't explain what was going on inside and became quite withdrawn (when not under the influence of booze or recreational drugs). On reflection, I had undiagnosed mental health issues but being a typical male of the time, I didn't tell anyone. I'm lucky and grateful to have a lovely wife and kids of my own and thankfully since becoming a parent, I've managed to completely change from my former hedonistic lifestyle to focusing on my family. While drinking these days is only once a week or fortnight, with regular abstinent spells, it still has the potential to cause me to worry on occasion. My excessive tendencies remain and I've often said I'd love to feel like I didn't need to drink to enjoy myself socially.

"As I've always been very wary of adding a regular drinking habit to binge drinking, I've used food as the more regular crutch. I often overeat and binge when feeling low but manage to handle my weight by exercising and fasting. It's been a permanent cycle and one that I hate. My siblings tell me I'm fine as they are heavier but it has always worried me. I know I'm eating to take me away from my problems and I want to free myself of this binge-shame cycle. Like the drinking, I have good spells where I don't binge but I'm often fighting the urge. I find it easier to be super strict and deny myself any treats due to my belief that I can't moderate but I know I'm denying myself one of the great pleasures of life.

"These coping mechanisms and others along the way have been used to deal with a deep underlying sadness, of feeling inferior and not good enough. I've done plenty of personal growth work which has helped but I know some deeper issues and beliefs still cause me to feel anxious around certain people and in group situations.

"So ultimately, I came to Geof hoping to be freed from these issues so that I could lead a much happier life."

Session One

"Geoff has a very relaxed and calm way about him and put me at ease from the moment I met him. We had a chat about his latest book and research which was fascinating and then we got down to the session. I relaxed back in the chair and away we went. I noticed a part of me that was cynical and tried to resist the process, I would be the one case that Geof wouldn't be able to help!

"I managed to accept this part of me and go with the flow. Sure enough, before too long I was in a semi-conscious state and following Geof's instruction as though on invisible strings.

"Geof guided me through a process where one by one I met all the family I had painful memories with. Geof helped me let out all my anger and resentment towards them and freed myself of the burden I had been carrying. At the same time, I forgave them and freed them of any of their sufferings. As I was listing all the negativity I wanted to be free from, I could feel a strong pressure building in my chest. This was followed by an even stronger release and as I breathed out through my nose the strong pressure and weight in my chest were released. The physical sensation of breathing in was powerful like I was drawing in fresh, purifying and energising air to replace the trapped, bad and now released energy.

"Next Geof guided me up a sweeping stone staircase to a warm red-panelled door. Though we went to a beautiful valley, with lush green grass, blue skies and white clouds dabbed across the horizon. I walked down to a lake where I saw the images of my mum and my dad, an emotional moment as they are both now passed. Geof again guided me through the release process of all the resentments, sadness, guilt and regrets I felt towards them. This was very emotional and powerful in different ways with mum and dad. There was more of an empathic sadness for my mum's suffering through her life and early death. With my dad, there was also empathy for his struggle but accompanied by a huge release of the pressure I had felt as a child from his sometimes menacing presence.

"The negative energy leaving my body reminded me of the scene in the movie The Green Mile where John Coffey would suck all the bad energy out of a person and release it into the sky or nearby like a black swarm. I told them I no longer wanted to carry the burden of these issues, of their issues but that I loved them and knew they did their best. I also freed them of the burden they were carrying. Again, I felt a great release of pressure in my chest as I let go of all the negativity and this was then replaced with a beautiful golden light which we bathed in together. It felt like pure love and I could have stayed there for a lot longer, free from all worries. To say it was a beautiful, cathartic moment doesn't do it justice but they are the closest words I can find right now.

"There are parts of the session where the memories are vague and distant and I have not put them all into words but it was a magical experience. The session was drawing to an end and Geof brought me back to the staircase and back up through the door. Soon Geof was counting down and bringing me back up to full consciousness and the room. When I opened my eyes to come back to the present, I thought I had been under for maybe half an hour or so. I was amazed when Geof told me ninety-five minutes had passed! It went so quickly. My state when I came out was one of mild euphoria and took me back to my teenage days on a mellow psychedelic trip. It was just a shame I had to rush off home to work! Geoff was brilliant and I can't wait for my second session."

Session Two

"The session began with Geof putting me into a relaxed state. I found my mind was a bit distracted again by a cynical, doubting voice that tried to resist the process. I was reassured by Geof's calm and the things that came up as he guided me along. Geof put me into a hypnotic state and asked me to visualise the familiar stone staircase that led to the red-panelled door, only this week we didn't go through the door. Next to the door was a bundle of glowing white light energy, a doorway or portal to the universe.

"Geof guided me through the portal and when I did, I was rushed forward through the universe. It sounds pretty wacky but as I travelled through, white and multi-coloured lights were flashing by and I felt completely relaxed with it all. We then arrived in what I think was the past and Geof asked me who I saw. Two images came to me, the first was a large, overweight man, with dark brown hair in a brown pin-striped suit and bowler-style hat. The second was an attractive fair-haired lady, dressed in simple 18th-century clothes and a bonnet-style hat. It felt like the man had his worries and struggled with his weight, finding comfort through food.

"The woman appeared sad in some hard-to-define way. I wasn't sure what their message for me was, the cynical part of me felt like I was making this stuff up and was distracting me but Geof led me through the process of releasing their negative energy. I pictured a dark grey swarm of negativity leaving my body and returning to them and that was replaced by a brilliant white light that shone from inside me and radiated out in all directions. The swarm of negative energy, now black then left them and was replaced with the same white light which freed them from their suffering.

"Next, we were travelling again back through the universe and we arrived in this state between places where there was nothing, only blackness and my consciousness. Geof spoke to my self-consciousness about the need to let me be free from the worries and concerns of the past. This felt like a powerful place, or state of mind, it was profound and very calm, a deep state of trance.

"Then, we were travelling again through the air to a tropical island. Surrounded by a clear blue sea, the island was lush and green. I walked through the grass and noticed the blue sky overhead. I'm writing this only an hour after the session and still, I can't remember all the details, other than it was a place of calm and peace. It's similar to a dream where sometimes you don't remember everything but just the feeling that is impressed upon you. Geof guided me back to the staircase and back up into the reality of the room. When asked how I felt, I said I didn't know but it was very different to the euphoria I felt on 'returning to the room' last week.

"On reflection, "mixed feelings" would be about right. I felt relaxed but disappointed that the session was over so quickly. I also had a feeling of doubt that this would work for me. Geof told me it was very rare for two people to be seen, which added fuel to the sneaky feeling I had that I was making stuff up! My analytical mind is constantly running and questioning things but Geof reassured me that the process would work regardless of my resistance."

Session Three

"After speaking to Geof throughout the week about my 'resistance' to the process, I'd followed his advice to judge by how I was feeling – and to be honest I had been feeling pretty positive. I hadn't felt any urge to drink at weekends which was a good sign and I was looking forward to the next session. We began as usual with Geof putting me into a hypnotic state as I relaxed back into the chair. We approached the familiar stone staircase and ascended to the red door. We went through the door into a field with the same lush, green grass and blue skies as in previous weeks.

"Geof asked me to look out for a building in the distance. Into focus came an old classical-style building set on its own. The building was a library and we approached and went into a room with tall, floor-to-ceiling bookcases. These were the kind of bookcases with vertical ladders on rails attached. There was a warm red Chesterfield-style leather armchair and table in the room. I went and sat in the chair.

"Geof took me back in time till I arrived in a jungle in South America. I was looking at a dark-haired man in the clothing of the time. It felt like the 14-1500's and the man, a colonist, was scared as though people were watching from the trees. I could feel his fear and my chest was tight. On reflection, I am from a southern Irish background and there is believed to be Spanish in the family line before that.

"Geof guided me through the process of releasing the fear and negativity as in previous weeks. The next thing I was back in the room and looking through an old book on the table. The book had a gilded red cover and was very thick. I opened the book and Geof asked me what I could see. It opened on a page with an image of my mum, a scene I remember as a child. I was taken into the picture with her and I felt her love but also her pain and her struggles.

"We connected and then released the pain we both felt which was replaced by a positive white light and energy. We repeated the process of looking through the book and my sister appeared. Before I knew it the session was over and I was taken back into full consciousness and the room feeling euphoric and buoyant."

Session Four

"In the week since the last session, I'd felt positive about things and so was looking forward to the session as usual. Another weekend had passed without any urge to drink and I was glad of waking on Saturday morning feeling fresh with no effects of the drink to deal with.

"We began the session in the usual way and after Geof had relaxed me and I was in hypnosis, we went up the steps to the door. This week it was a deeper blue colour but in the same panelled style as previously. On the other side of the door, I found myself in the same familiar field with rich green grass and blue skies. In the distance, I could see a huge Oak tree and Geof said I should head for it. Underneath the tree, there was an unrolled treasure map on aged paper. There was nothing on the map as a clue to what was next but the tree seemed to hold some unknown significance.

"With no clue on the map to focus on, Geof took me back in time to meet my ancestors and I arrived in what seemed the very distant past, around the 600s. I had arrived at night time, the sky was inky black and the stars were bright. I seemed to be embodied in an ancient ancestor as I could see my bottom half and feet in first-person view. I was wearing simple clothing at the time - my legs were exposed below the hips and I had leather sandals on. I looked around and out at the dark wall trees on all sides. They seemed to carry a threat, it was like I was being watched and there was imminent danger set to spring out from the trees at any time.

"The night turned into a beautiful bright day and I felt more at ease. I could see mud huts and I approached one and went inside. There was a woman and a child who had their backs on me. They had dark hair and skin and were sitting on the floor. She was preparing food and neither mother nor the child was aware of my presence. I had the sense they were my family but there was the same feeling of threat and danger from my wife who too, it seemed, was worried about an attack.

"Geof took me through the same release process as in previous weeks to free myself and my ancestors from these trapped feelings. I felt a weight lifted from me as the bad energy was released from me and my ancestors and that was replaced by the energising white light energy. We felt the love between us and I could have stayed in the light a lot longer than I did. I spoke to Geof about this at the end as I'd felt like this every week. Geof said we should listen to this signal and we would in the remaining weeks.

"We travelled forward in time again and returned to the field and back under the tree. I wasn't sure what the tree's message was but I know I had some connection with it. Geof suggested I hug the tree which I did and it felt good. We then returned to the reality of the room and another session had flown by.

"In my normal conscious state, I love trees and am often drawn to the beauty and scale and love spending time in nature. I'll be pondering the significance of this week's session."

Session Five

"I chatted to Geof before we started about how I'd been feeling pretty good in the week since the last session. I told Geof my only concern was the ongoing question I had about my career. While I don't mind aspects of my work, I don't think it's my calling and I've long wanted to find my element.

By element, I mean the sweet spot of being something I love but can also do well.

"I've often felt that was something more practical and not a sedentary desk job like my current role. I love working with wood for example, I also have that ongoing connection with trees and have wondered whether this was some kind of signpost. The challenge is finding a way that allows us to maintain the comfortable family life we enjoy but also brings me that fulfilment I'm seeking.

"We got into the session and after Geof had hypnotised me, he spoke to my higher self about what I was seeking. Geof asked my higher self to provide the guidance and direction I was looking for in terms of my career and interests and suggested to my unconscious mind that the universe would guide me towards finding my element.

"Next I was facing the familiar stone steps and walking up to the heavy-looking, navy blue panelled door. There was an old brass key in the door which was quite ornate and beautiful. I went through the door and as I closed it behind me, I took the key out to keep with me. We were in a field, with green grass underfoot and blue skies above.

"I looked down at my clothes and I was wearing a tunic and tight-fitting pants, like a sailor from the 1700s might wear. In the distance, I could see a man. I couldn't make out what he looked like so I came closer. The man had a strong presence and appeared to be some kind of native American Indian chief. He was strong and silent and felt like he could potentially be a threat. I felt wary of him.

"We were then transported through time to see the sailor's family. I was looking at my wife and child as my wife was preparing food. We were in a kind of simple hut and my wife sat stirring a pan of soup. As she began serving it into wooden bowls, I noticed there was sadness around the family. There had been a terrible loss, they had lost a child to disease and they were powerless to help him.

"We went through the process of releasing the sadness from us all. I no longer wished to carry this burden around and neither did the family. The negativity left our bodies in a black haze and was replaced with a beautiful white light. We bathed in that light, it enriched every cell in our body and energised us. We felt love for one another and as we departed, they had a message for me to trust myself.

"Then we revisited the Indian chief. His strong, imposing presence made sense to me now as I realised he had felt threatened and under attack. His homeland had been invaded by a violent, murdering enemy, the colonists and I was part of this invading force. The sailor had carried guilt for being part of the invasion and as we stood face to face, we understood each other clearly. Once again, we repeated the process of releasing the burden from us both and replaced the negativity with a bath of white light. We were left feeling energised and loving towards each other. The chief's departing message for me was to trust my instincts.

"I then walked back up the steps and through the door. As I closed it behind me, I took the key out of my pocket and left it in the door. I was then back in the reality of the room with Geoff, energised and full of positivity."

Session Six

"I was looking forward to my final session and had been feeling generally positive since the last session. We chatted about my career change plans and possible ways to set the wheels in motion as it's become clear to me how much I need a change. Geof said it was draining my life energy doing something I don't like and this resonated with me as I know how energised I feel when I do something practical that I enjoy.

"Geof went through the usual steps of putting me into a hypnotic state and I felt deeply relaxed. We went up the stone stairs to the red-panelled door and through. On the other side, I stood in a meadow with beautiful blue skies above and lush grass underfoot. Geof said there was a crystal here somewhere and to find it. I could see the oak tree from previous weeks and underneath it was a palm-sized clear white crystal. I picked it up and then it created a glowing white light doorway, like a portal.

"We passed through the light and when we got through to the other side it was night time. The sky was black, the stars were bright and I was standing on soil. Overhead were the spirits of my ancestors, circling me as glowing light. My spirit began to leave my body, to raise to them, leaving me standing below.

"One man stood out, he was dressed in 17th-century clothing with a tricorn hat and wig. I could feel his sense of worry, fear and sadness. No words were spoken. Geof took us through the process of releasing the negative energy that had passed down my ancestral line from him to me. The swarm of black negative energy first left my body, then the man's and was accompanied by my sigh as it was released.

"It was replaced by a beautiful white, energising light that I could feel healing every cell in my body. The light also freed the man from his unhappiness. As we left the man, released from his burdens I felt compassion towards him.

"The next thing there was a folded letter in my hands. I opened it up but it was blank inside. I understood this to mean my future was there for the making. I had the freedom to make different choices and head in any direction I chose. I felt incredibly relaxed throughout today's session and as the session drew to a close, I was taken back to the room in a state of complete peace and calm.

"I've enjoyed the last six weeks with Geoff and feel I have gained a lot. It's an on-going process and things are still unfolding for me. I'll be making some changes to my direction in life and am excited to discover what the future holds."

Chapter 18: James' Story

Let's find out why James chose to visit me in the first place. James, who was struggling with depression, worry, tension, discontent, and the fear of being judged, turned to alcohol as a means of evading his problems and escaping his life. He feels he is not good enough.

James, who is now 33 years old, was bereaved by the death of his brother, who took his own life at the age of 26. He is a family man today, married and has a beautiful son.

Session One

"I had a few doubts in my mind but would always class myself as an open-minded person. I had heard about hypnotherapy in the past from friends but never gave it a second thought!

"My problem with binge drinking and bouts of depression for the past few years led me to reach out to Geof. We discussed my fear of being judged by other people which was holding me back in my personal and professional life.

"The session started with Geof bringing me into a deep trance, we went through what I can only describe as diving deeper through stages of my consciousness until after several levels. I was down in the depths of my mind with Geoff at the wheel.

"Geof took me back to an event which happened in high school, this event still had a lasting impact on my life.

"During my teenage years, I struggled with home life which impacted my friendships in high school. Eventually, my "friends" told me they didn't want me around anymore. I was holding onto the dark/negative energy of this event.

"Geof guided me through facing these dark forces head-on through the people involved in the incident, this was an extremely emotional journey where I unloaded my dark energy, and then replaced it with the light of love from my family. I began with a complete and utter hatred of these people, by the end of this section, I had gone from hatred to pity to complete nothingness around the event.

"Geof took me to see a younger version of myself before the high school event and I told him how much he is loved by all those around him. I told my younger self that no matter how much life gets bad, he will always be loved and I will always protect him. My younger self was ultimately absorbed back into me, a much-needed reunion.

"As the session continued, Geof guided me back through time starting within my mother's womb with my twin sister. I could feel the close maternal bond with my mother and the love she had for me and my sister.

"Next up was the first time I walked; I relived a memory of me walking from my mother to my father in the living room of my childhood home wearing just a nappy! The love from my mother and father led me to tears.

"We then travelled to my first birthday, where I was in a flat of some sort with my mother and two other women. The whole area and the two ladies felt so familiar, I felt as if I knew them but couldn't put my finger on who they were. I was wearing a red outfit and remembered a small chocolate cake.

"Our next destination was my 21st birthday. I was on holiday in Greece with my friends. Geoff was continually prompting me to hold on to these feelings of love & happiness.

"This is where the journey went to another level for me! Geoff told me to picture a set of stairs. I could see a grand set of stairs with a golden bannister leading upwards. Upon reaching the top of the stairs, Geoff asked me to picture a door.

"What I can only describe as a cosmic portal appeared before me, it was a doorframe-shaped light piercing towards me. When I looked in, I could only see the vast universe. Geof told me to enter the door. I didn't feel any fear of stepping into the portal. Below is an image that closely matches what I saw.

"When I got through, it felt as if I had gone into another plane of consciousness mind-blowing. There was amazing scenery, a clear blue sky, a vast green meadow, enormous mountains and a pathway down to a lake. Geoff told me to follow the path and I would meet my brother who had taken his own life 7 years ago.

"The emotion of this overwhelmed me at this point. My brother said, "how're you, mate!?" I introduced him to my wife and 2-year-old son.

"My grandparents who had passed on appeared, the first thing my grandfather Paul said to me was "Wow, the size of you!" as I'm 6ft4. I introduced my son and wife to my grandparents; they were so happy and playing with my son. They told me that they were there for me and they would always watch over me and my family.

"All while this was unfolding the portal that I had pictured earlier remained at the beginning of the path, waiting for me to return.

"Slowly my family from the other side left and went into the beautiful environment before me. Geof then guided me back through the portal and back up to my normal level of consciousness.

"When I awoke my mind was completely blown by what had just happened, I felt a wide range of emotions such as happiness, sadness and everything in between! Even slightly nauseous.

"The room felt different from when I had first come into it, it felt like my body was absorbing positive energy from the atmosphere. I felt like I had a hole in my chest where the negative and dark emotions had left me and new positive atoms were entering.

"The session then ended and it's safe to say I had never in my life experienced such an intensely emotional journey of healing.

"On speaking to James after just one session he said he feels fantastic.

Session Two

"In the week after my first session with Geof, I was left feeling renewed. I finally started to feel like my demons from my childhood had started to dissipate. My drinking had reduced dramatically also.

"Before my second session, I was quite nervous but excited also, I also wanted to learn more about this new world that Geof had introduced me to!

"Geof began the session by once again changing my state of consciousness; he had informed me earlier that he would be speaking to my higher self today. Once I was under, Geof summoned my higher self by asking him if he was present, could David's right middle finger raise slowly... And it did!!

"Geof then spoke with my higher self, who had been protecting me for all of my life from past traumas, and told him that I need to be free. I do not require protection anymore, I need to live my own life. I and the other self were then cleansed, and I instantly felt a feeling of closure after this had happened. None of this experience was unpleasant, it was like meeting an old friend.

"The next part is where it got crazy! Geof told me to think of a set of stairs with a ball of energy at the top, this ball of energy was a portal. I stepped through the portal and slowly left the earth until I was staring back down over the vast oceans and mountains of our amazing planet.

"In the middle of space, was another door. I went through a void of nothingness where I could only feel peace. There was then another door which I entered. This was a doorway back to one of my ancestors.

"Geof asked me several questions once I met my ancestor:
· Is it a female or male? – Female I replied.
· How old is she? - In her 30's
· What year is it? - 1600's
· What is she wearing? - She was dressed like a Victorian maid."

"Geof then asked me what she is feeling. At this point, an overwhelming sense of sorrow took over me and my eyes began to fill with tears. I began quite emotional and told Geof that this poor girl was feeling complete and utter loneliness, rejection and abandonment. Her story was being radiated through me, she had become pregnant out of wedlock and her family had turned her away.

"I spoke with this lady and told her that her protection wasn't needed anymore, I wasn't going to live her life and she needs to be free as do I.

"This part of the session blew my mind, Geof had said prior that we would be meeting one of my ancestors and I sort of laughed it off but WOW. I did not expect to have the level of connection with this person and feel such raw emotions as I did!

"In the next part of the session, Geof guided me back through space and time, to a desert island. I can only describe this place as a traditional desert island with beige sand and trees etc. Except the sky was the vast grand universe, it felt like another realm. While on the island, there was a rainbow. I followed it until its end where I found two items. These were a piece of paper with writing I couldn't understand and an old brass key.

"Geof asked me, what does the writing say? I just couldn't read it, Geof conjured a magnifying glass that enable me to read what was written down... Geof asked once more. What does the writing say? It said, "THERE IS MORE". Geof asked, what does that mean, the words that I could only find where there is more than life, there is more than what we see. I couldn't believe what I was saying.

"Geof told me we were going to leave this place now, but to check if there were any more items I had missed. An old wooden school chair appeared; it was calling me to sit in it.

"As I was leaving this strange and wonderful place, I took everything I had found with me back to the portal.

"The session concluded and Geof awoke me from the trance I sat up and grabbed Geof's shoulder and said, "Geof! That was insane!" I felt such excitement and confusion about what had just happened. A weight lifted from my mind once more and an intrigue for the next session to find out what these items meant!

"Geof said we would be visiting "The Library" in our next session, which I couldn't wait for!"

Session Three

"Before this session, I had my usual anticipation for Geof's session. He had previously told me that we would be visiting ``The Library" this week.

"Geof began the session and once I was under, we began the journey to the library. Once again picturing a set of stairs with a door at the top. At the top was this amazing old library which held thousands of books.

"I can still see it now in my mind! Geof then asked me if I could see anything, and an old wooden chair appeared. I sat in the chair, and it took me back in time to visit an ancestor. In the previous session, I briefly met a lady from the 1600s. This time, I revisited her!

"Geof asked me what she was wearing – she looked like a maid. How old was she? - Late 20's. What was she feeling? - A deep sense of shame, regret and loss.

"Geof then said, what are YOU wearing?" After looking down I was dressed in a brown formal suit with brown leather shoes on. Geof continued, who are you to this lady? I don't know how to explain this but I just KNEW who I was and could sense that I was the lady's father and all of the emotions he was carrying.

"The young lady had got pregnant outside of marriage and disgraced the family. Her father was deeply torn between turning his back on his daughter and standing by her...

Ultimately due to the total shame the daughter had brought on the family, the father had cast her out and stopped any other family members from keeping contact. Cut ties.

"This was a horrible decision that he had to make. I could feel the regret and sorrow but he felt like he had no other choice in the matter. It was extremely emotional... But he and his wife never spoke to her again.

"Geof then instructed me to "step out" of this man, tell him that I can't live his life any longer and his issues are his own. They are not mine to hold on too. The fear of what other people think of me and the fear of being judged was coming through via this man.

"Geof guided me into the Lady's future, to which I felt an overwhelming sense of happiness and peace. She now had an 8-year-old boy and was living somewhere remote with her partner – content. This gave me such a great sense of peace within, knowing that even though her whole family had turned their backs on her, she made it through the other side!

"We then returned to the library; Geof asked me if there were any items that had appeared. I replied, yes – a beautiful golden pen. Geof again asked me what did the pen do or signify? I replied this is a pen that has the power to rewrite my destiny.

"As those words left my mouth, I was overcome with a tsunami of emotion and began crying at this realisation that I had been holding onto the notion that I couldn't change what people thought of me and things would never change.

"Since a very young age, I had always felt as though I didn't fit in with people like I was somehow different from the crowd. Geof told me to put the pen in my pocket and keep it with me forever and always remember that it is with me. Geof then began to bring me back to normal consciousness.

"Once I awoke, Geof asked me how I was feeling. I felt a wave of different emotions. The confusion is the main one!

"I said to Geof that from the previous session, I thought my ancestor that I was holding onto was the young lady, but this week had revealed it was her father!

"All of the feelings of being judged by people were his! I'm still trying to get my head around what happened in this session but I needed it and couldn't be more grateful to Geof. Geof and I laughed as this was only the third session! Another mind-blowing one at that!"

Session Four

"This was my fourth session with Geof, by this point my drinking had noticeably lowered not having had an alcoholic drink in two weeks. Which was unheard of before coming to see Geof.

"Every week I come to the sessions and don't think that anything can surprise me more, and every week I'm proven wrong!

"Geof started the session in his usual way and brought me down into a lower consciousness. I pictured a set of stairs, followed them up and went through a door with a blinding light behind it. Once inside, Geof guided me back in time to a yet-to-be-discovered ancestor.

"Geof asked:
Where are you? - At a train yard, I replied.
How old are you? - around 12 years old
Are you alone? - I'm with friends, playing.
What year is it? - early 1800's
What can you see? - Train tracks all around, coal, lots of coal in the back of old unused storage carts
What is your name? -Peter Coogan I replied."

"Geof then asked me about the place, did it have any significance? Has something happened there? I replied it was just me and my friends playing. Nothing bad had happened, children shouldn't be here but that's only because it's unsafe for kids.

"Geof asked:
What does your father do for a living? - He works on the ships.
What does your mother do? - she cleans."

"I said that if mum and dad knew I was playing here, they would batter me!

"Geof then took me forward into Peter's life. Now he is about 20 years old. He was arguing with his fiance. Geof asked what the argument was about, I told him that his fiance was planning on leaving Peter. She was in love with another man. The feelings I could feel coming through were intense feelings of dread, loss, rejection and insignificance.

"I spoke to the lady and Peter and told them I couldn't hold onto their burden any longer, they wouldn't live through me any longer. We were all cleansed by a mighty golden light which destroyed the dark energy.

"Geof then guided me back to the door, but before leaving, there was a golden globe next to it. I looked inside the globe. Smoke started to emit from it and the words "explore" came out. When I saw this, I got the instant feeling that it was telling me to explore as much of life as possible!

"Geof then brought me back to speak to him. Once again I was lost for words. When I originally came to Geoff it was for the fear of being judged and drinking too much. I didn't tell him that myself and my wife had been having issues due to my drinking which resonated with my ancestor. I got emotional when I explained this to Geof but felt an amazing sense of relief also. Another end to an amazingly insane session!

"The link between James and his ancestor Peter was forcing him to drink in this life which generated a problem with the relationship in his marriage today. I'm here to say it is not his fault and he is not to blame. He was reliving the feelings of his ancestor Peter.

Session Five

"I was still trying to get my head around the last session and how this young man called Peter had been pushing his wife away and I had been doing the same and turning to alcohol.

"Geof had told me this week's session would involve the lost key so I was excited to see where these adventures of my mind would lead too!

"The session began in the normal way of Geof making me dive deeper and deeper into my mind. Geof told me to picture a set of stairs, at the top of the stairs was a fantastic golden door with a key In it.

"I turned the key, opened the door and walked through into an amazing white light. I then turned around, closed the door, locked it and took the key with me.

"Geof said we were now going to visit one of my ancestors and after a few moments I would be somewhere.

"Geof asked, is it night or day – Night I replied.
If you look down, what is under your feet? Grass
Do you know this place? No
If you look forwards, what can you see? A small village – a fishing village
What is this place to you? Home, I responded

What year is it? Feels like the early 1900s

How old are you? I'm a 28-year-old man."

"I began to explain to Geof the sense of history that was rushing through to me from the person I had become. The young man was a fisherman and was coming home after being in prison for quite some time. He was headed straight for the local pub to meet somebody.

"Once in the pub, he met with an older man who felt like a mentor figure. There were moments of happiness and even love shared.

"Geof asked, is there a girl waiting for you? Yes, I replied, but something has happened between them. The young man isn't with his girlfriend anymore. She moved on after he went to prison.

"After the pub, the young man left and headed to his mother's home who wasn't expecting him, he embraced his mother with so much love. Emotions of guilt and shame were coming through also around the fact he had left his mother alone for so long. The young man's mother hated him working as a fisherman, the sense of worry was very potent.

"It was now the following day, and the young man's past girlfriend knocked at the door. They embraced each other with so much love. But the young man knew he couldn't be with her any longer as she had a new family now. I could feel the sense of regret from the young lady but it was over, no chance of anything happening again. It was too late.

"At this point, Geof instructed me to step out of the young man and confront him and the girl. Tell them I wouldn't live their lives anymore. Their issues are theirs, not mine to hold onto and relive. We were then cleansed by a ray of light which destroyed the negative energy of this memory.

"After the cleansing happened, Geof guided me back through the village and to the golden door. I used the key to open it and returned to reality.

"After every one of these sessions is over, I always struggle to process what has just happened as I can't explain it, but the experiences and emotions that come through are so real!

"Since the beginning of the sessions, it feels like layers of insecurities are being removed. It's becoming clearer and clearer that there are many ancestors from my past who have been impacting my life in the present and have confronted them and removed the negative energy that I'm holding. I already feel my life has improved. I'm drinking 90% less than I was, my confidence has rocketed and my relationship with my wife has never been better!"

Session Six

"It was my final session with Geoff, and as always there was a sense of nervousness and excitement about what I was going to see.

"The session began as normal and Geof guided me into lower states of consciousness, he asked me to imagine a set of stairs. A golden set of stairs appeared with a light at the top. I walked up the stairs and entered the light. It always feels as though I've stepped into some sort of other dimensions at this part of every session.

"Once through, Geof asked me to relay information about where I was. I was on a beach with golden sand beneath my feet, and a glorious blue sky. There was a young girl aged around 10 who was also there. Geof explained that this was a guide/somebody who has been watching over me.

"I walked for some time on the beach until I approached a huge old tree! The tree has a hole in the centre of it. I reached into the hole and pulled out a crystal.

"When I looked at the crystal, what I can only describe as a cloud of ancestors began to float above me. Geof informed me at this point that an ancestor that was closely linked to my life would present itself. Immediately, a young man from a previous session whose fiancé was leaving him appeared. But this time so much more information was coming through from him, about his life. I could feel that his father was an alcoholic. He also struggled with alcohol, which was a contributing factor to why he had pushed his fiancé away.

"I felt all of the emotions of shame, anxiety and the want to change from this person. This was also very similar to the emotions I've felt in the past with my drinking problems.

"I confronted this gentleman and his father, explaining that I cannot live their lives any longer. I need to be free of their problems. The negative energy left my body and was purged by a golden light which covered all of us.

"After this point, I returned the crystal to the tree, Geof asked if the little girl was still there. I replied, yes.

"Geof began asking me about this young girl, who was she? She is my great x 5 grandmother. I could feel that this was her purest form and that this woman has a very young soul. She was dressed which was appeared to be Victorian clothing.

"Geof asked me about her life, at this point I became very emotional in the session as I could sense that she had a very hard life with much sadness and loss but also with so much love and happiness. During this, the little girl kept telling me – Never lose the child in you... Never lose the child in you. I found this so shocking! But I understand it also, I have a very "serious" job and take my responsibilities of looking after my wife and son very seriously also.

"I knew the young girl was telling me to make sure I keep the childish side of me alive as I grow older. I spoke with my grandmother of many generations back and thanked her for protecting me and looking out for me. I then began to tell her that I'm now fine and don't need protecting moving forwards, I need to live my own life. This was again extremely emotional; I can feel the connection to these people and the whole range of emotions.

"Geof then began the process of taking me back and the session concluded. Geof asked me how I feel and as always, I replied that I was still trying to process it all, it blows my mind... every single session... I walk away and think that I couldn't be more surprised but with each session, something happens that I can't explain.

"When I first came to see Geof, I was suffering from depression, alcoholism, general sadness and anxiety. Since the sessions have come to an end. My drinking has been reduced by around 95%. A certain change has taken place within me where I no longer feel constrained by what other people think of me, a sense of freedom. Generally, all around I feel much happier and closer to my wife and son. I can't thank Geoff enough for the journeys he has taken me on.

"I've had the opportunity to reunite with my brother who sadly passed away, and various members of my ancestors. What an experience! Thank you so much, Geoff."

I plan on keeping an eye on James over the next year to demonstrate how effective inherited Therapy and the Loveday Method are; and how they can release the traumas that people are going through so they can find true happiness and inner peace.

Chapter 19: Ryan's Journey.

Session One: The Journey

"Came to Geoff's home, welcomed in, sat, and chatted about things such as mood, how I had been and what I expected from the sessions.

"Had been feeling down in previous days compared to how I had been feeling in the previous days and weeks, however still much improved from when this episode began around 5/5 weeks previously.

"We talked about the process and reiterated what I hoped to achieve from the session, HAPPINESS, and spoke about the job I do and how it can be stressful but rewarding, the stresses of family life with a two-year-old son and another on the way.

"Spoke about intrusive thoughts that have crept back in but felt like I was controlling them better and realised they don't belong to me, we talked about inherited emotions, how antidepressants are not the answer if they can be avoided, me wanting to go back in time to 6/7 weeks previous where I was content and living in the moment, not overthinking anything just being happy and content. I just want a happy simple life for me and my family.

"After chatting I got comfortable in the chair, music was played, blinds closed, and Geoff tested my hypnosis which was working so we commenced.

"I put both my hands on the arms of the chair, and Geoff told me the points he would touch my arms and forehead etc, session started and here is what I remember, I will try to get the order as best I can.

"Left hand was for positive aspects of my life and happy thoughts I had, such as my son, my girlfriend, and family friends, started to rise when prompted to think of these nice moments.

"Right hand was linked to negative moments and emotions, and the hand started to rise asked Geoff to get rid of these emotions and feelings, to throw them away and release them from me.

"Hands slowly rise and come together to join in the middle of my chest. In the time memories of visions I saw included, looking up at the sky when younger, stars, barefoot, and images of my mother, became emotional after talking and thinking about her and what she has been through in the past few years.

"Asked to remember myself walking for the first time, I saw what I thought was myself walking in a nappy, not sure if the baby was me or not, seeing memory from almost a 4th wall perspective.

"Asked to remember a birthday party again seen from the 4th wall, square table in what may have been old house eating room kids and people round but couldn't make out a face, was maybe wearing a green and red patch shirt

"Asked to remember when born, looking up at mother threw babies eyes feeling love and protection

"Asked to remember inside the womb, felt like I was inside the womb but not sure if projection, felt almost lava - lampesque, maybe feeling of love worry stress, hard to tell.

"Asked to remember happy memories from youth, remembering playing in street in summer holidays was hot, bowl heads, with Raymond, felt happiness and innocence.

"Remembered playing on PlayStation in my room; die hard 2 games with Raymond. Both real memories

"Asked at some point to go to the three-year-old me who had worried from mother, to tell him everything would be okay, and I would take care of him and that no one was to blame. Not sure why did this occur.

"Still felt moments of negativity during this session, some intrusive thoughts creeping in etc.

"Asked about the staircase, the staircase was concrete and led up to a door which was coloured green, don't know why green.

"Opened the door to what Geoff described as a valley, with lovely green fields and waterfalls and hills. Described a path leading down to a lake where Fernanda and Leonardo were sat

"As walking down the path a figure was waiting on the path, almost a shadow, Geoff explained grandparents, faces became clear. Seeing through my eyes, the faces of both sets of grandparents were visible and interchangeable almost

"Repeated a mantra said by Geoff about forgiving them and myself but that this stress and darkness didn't belong to me, expelled black mist/cloud from myself and replaced it with bright light from grandparents.

"This happened several times when the light was golden silver.

"Introduced my grandparents to Fernanda and Leonardo, they told me I would be okay and that everything would work out, filling me with more light.

"At this time I was asked to bring hands together and squeeze when positive influence was described.

"Left grandparents, everyone wished each other well and we left with feelings of love and happiness.

"Came back emotional and trying to make sense of what had occurred.

"Hard to figure out Geoff said 24/48 hours healing would be strange.

"Sunday and Monday were up and down but grew into the days

"Going to the match Monday evening was good, good to get some normality, but still had some intrusive thoughts but less than the week before.

"Tuesday was a better day than the previous days, tired still of some negativity but less than the previous."

Session Two: The Universe.

"I Met Geoff he welcomed me into his home, I sat and we chatted about how I had been feeling since the first session. The first couple of days had been up and down, but from Wednesday onwards had grown into the week and was feeling better Wednesday Thursday Friday.

"Saturday morning, I had some trepidation, almost not sure why maybe nerves about the session or tiredness or maybe everything combined. We talked about the previous session and how and what today's session would entail spoke about my job with Geoff reminding me I am a good person who does a good job and takes care of people.

"Again we started the process of relaxing in the chair dimming the lights and playing relaxing music, went through the stages of becoming relaxed and hypnotised, focused on counting backwards from 100 while focusing on my left and right hands rising from the arms on the chair, thinking about the happy times and the important people in my life, eventually with my hands resting on my chest and being relaxed, here's what I remember in the best order I can remember.

"After becoming relaxed we visualised a ball of light almost golden and silver coloured.

"I stepped into the ball and it started to climb higher and higher into the sky the blue sky.

"Eventually we climbed higher so that I could see the earth from below, looking up I could see bright stars.

"We started to travel in this ball at a fast pace until we found a circular doorway that looked different from the rest of the area.

"We went through this door into what seemed a very black still area, no stars.

"This it was said was an almost dimension that shouldn't have been available for us to reach.

"As we further travelled we saw another doorway that opened into a time that seemed to be around the 1920/the 30s but may have been earlier

"There I encountered a man in what seemed to be maybe a shipyard almost working type of area.

"The man who I came to see was the maybe mid-30s with a floppy type of side part hair and sharp features, handsome, slim, and maybe around 6ft maybe slightly less

"He was dressed in a short-sleeved shirt and trousers almost work-like attire, not a fashion statement.

"He seemed like a man who had worry and sadness in him, I was not sure of the man's situation or his life as I had never seen him before.

"He seemed a kind and decent person.

"Like the first session we repeated the mantra that his pain suffering guilt etc wasn't mine to take on and it didn't belong to me, I deserved to live a happy and content life.

"I was told to dispel any bad feelings and guilt pain etc from myself.

"I felt it come out of the palm of my hands as a black mist type of substance it wasn't solid.

"Repeated the mantra, while also dispelling any bad energy and pain from him.

"Felt after this experience the man was then full of happiness and contentment, we left on good terms with well wishes and happiness for the future.

"Taken back into a ball and travelled again until we saw an island.

"Landed lightly on the island, was barefoot in the sand looked round and there were lovely green and colourful plants and almost jungle-type feel.

"There were buildings in the distance with a path leading through the jungle.

"Geoff talked about realigning chakras and as I was walking through the jungle Geoff was telling me about the different chakra parts and colours.

"Example was a red tingle of colour illuminating the jungle when discussing the root chakra and then orange, green etc as I walked further on.

"Then when all the colours had been discussed and felt we got to the end of the rainbow.

"Geoff asked what was waiting there and I told him it felt like happiness not in words or a gift more like a feeling.

"Geoff told me to take it with me, came back to the ball of light and energy and departed.

"Came back the way we came and then came back, with a feeling of relaxation and contentment.

"Spoke with Geoff about what I felt and saw, felt good afterwards, felt much more in tune with it all than in the previous week and feel like progress is being made and believe this process will help me."

Session Three: The Library.

"Again the session started similarly to the others, Geoff invited me into his home and we chatted about how I was doing, and what the family and work were like.

"Geoff had told me the previous week that our next session would be in the library which I was looking forward to participating in.

"The hypnosis started with Geoff putting me into a relaxing state like the previous weeks.

"Once I was relaxed and hypnotised how tall to imagine myself travelling in a ball of golden light climbing high through the clouds and driving higher and higher through to space.

"After travelling for a while we settle down on what seemed to be an island, while walking through the island came upon a staircase that led up to a door.

"The door was thick mahogany colour, old fashioned and sturdy with a round knob as the handle.

"I went through to a building of what seemed to be a library. It had spiral staircases and rows of books.

"It was light but at the same time had an old rich type of history feel to it, almost like a mahogany feel to the environment.

"I felt like I was around early to mid-20in s in this scenario, I was barefoot with jeans and a T-shirt on.

"I was then guided to a door to another room and on entering I was surprised as it reminded me of something like a Japanese garden, with a neat array of several plants and squares of smooth shiny black stone going from one end of what seemed to be a shallow pool.

"This was surprising knowledge or interest in this type of room so for it to be there was interesting to me.

"At the end of the room was a door that I passed through which led me through to another room, this room was much different to the last one.

"This room was almost like an old-fashioned room which reminded me of a study, again with mahogany and old wood type of feel to it.

"It had a large table and large mantel piece with an old fashioned fireplace with large windows which gave light to the whole room.

"Leaning on the mantelpiece was what seemed like a large man who was fairly tall and well built, he was dressed very smart and what seemed to be a tweed-type blazer with a shirt and tie.

"When entering the room this person had his back toward me, but while he looked and seemed authoritative and stern I realised he was a good, nice person with a good aura coming from him.

"Maybe he was some sort of guardian of the library, he had an aura of power and control about him.

"He did however remain with his back to me for most of the conversation and I didn't get to see his face.

"After getting closer to him again Like in the first session we repeated the mantra that his pain suffering guilt etc wasn't mine to take on and it didn't belong to me, I deserved to live a happy and content life.

"I was told to dispel any bad feelings and guilt pain etc from myself.

"I felt it come out of the palm of my hands as a black mist type of substance it wasn't solid.

"I was then engulfed in a golden light similar to the other times that made me feel warm safe and happy, after this me and the keeper said our goodbyes and we both went with feelings of respect and contentment.

"As I was leaving the room there was a red important looking book on the table as I was leaving with my name written in gold letters on the front.

"I was asked by Geoff to open a page at a random number which for me was number 7; again I don't know why number 7.

"Was told that this is the beginning of my happy future and a new beginning. On the way-out Geoff asked if was there anything for me by the door and there was a box wrapped with paper and ribbons almost like an over-the-top wrapped kid's present.

"I was told to take it and was asked what I would like to be inside it, I asked for happiness and contentment, and I then left the room.

"I went back through the Japanese-themed room into the spiral library with the luxurious chairs, back through the door and down the staircase and left the place I was.

"Geoff then brought me around and we proceeded to talk about the experience that had occurred.

"It was only when looking back and talking the experience over with my girlfriend that I realised the bookkeeper/ librarian in the study may have been an older version of myself.

"How this is possible I don't know and maybe it wasn't it was just a vibe/ feeling that I felt afterwards.

"Starting to feel progress is coming and these sessions can help me going forward, Geoff reminds me the process takes time and that everything will work out."

Session Four: The Treasure Map.

"Came to Geoff's home, welcomed in, sat, and chatted about things such as mood, how I had been feeling how work was going, about my girlfriend and her belief in spirituality and how she was taught growing up in Brazil and how much of a massive help and rock she had been for me through this difficult period.

"The hypnosis started with Geoff putting me into a relaxing state like the previous weeks.

"Left hand was for positive aspects of my life and happy thoughts I had, such as my son, my girlfriend, and family friends, started to rise when prompted to think of these nice moments.

"Right hand was linked to negative moments and emotions, and the hand started to rise asked Geoff to get rid of these emotions and feelings, to throw them away and release them from me.

"Asked to count back from 100 and throw those numbers away after saying them out loud. Hands slowly rise and come together to join in the middle of my chest.

"After becoming relaxed we visualised a ball of light almost golden and silver coloured. I stepped into the ball and it started to climb higher and higher into the sky into the blue sky. Eventually, we climbed higher so that I could see the earth from below, looking up I could see bright stars

"We started to travel in this ball at a fast pace until we found a circular doorway that looked different from the rest of the area.

"We went through this door into what seemed a very black still area, no stars.

"This it was said was an almost dimension that shouldn't have been available for us to reach.

"Eventually we have seen and landed on an island-type place that I have visited in previous sessions.

"The island began with a beach, which led into a forest-type area with a large building in the distance.

"I was told by Geoff that I was looking for a treasure map which would in turn lead me where I wanted to go.

"It may sound cliché but after walking further into the forest/ jungle I found the map next to a palm tree-type tree that I had seen in my previous sessions.

"There I found the map and it was a simple map with few landmarks but had dots leading a path of where I should go.

"I followed the map and eventually came upon a sort of hut type of house that was sort of built into the floor. There was a door but the rest of the house was sort of built into the dirt.

"The door was green and welcoming, and I entered. When I entered it was different to what I expected, as when I entered it was almost like a native American type of vibe.

"It was dark and there was a raging fire in the middle that was controlled coming out of a circular fire pit. It was shadowy and dark, but the flame gave the room an orange glow.

"It felt tribal and almost as if there should be a shaman present, a person was sitting opposite whose face was obscured due to the shadow but from time to time could get a glance due to the orange glow.

"After getting closer to him again Like in the first session we repeated the mantra that his pain suffering guilt etc. wasn't mine to take on and it didn't belong to me, I deserved to live a happy and content life.

"I was told to dispel any bad feelings and guilt pain etc. from myself.

"I felt it come out of the palm of my hands as a black mist type of substance it wasn't solid.

"This time however I burned this negative darkness away with the fire pit. I felt I had full control of the fire pit and it was there to aid me with my journey.

"It was almost like any negative or intrusive thought I had I could hold it over the fire and burn it away, the person opposite me gave off a feeling of secureness and safety even though we never conversed or interacted together.

"I felt great whilst in this environment which is strange as I have never had any interest or involvement with that type of subject before."

There have been many stories and journeys of the many people I've been able to help; these are just a few. The Loveday Method is so effective that the outcomes have been quite remarkable. After reading you are now beginning to realise; these feelings we are holding onto were there before we were born.

PART TWO

Chapter 20: Transgenerational Trauma

The concept of trauma being passed down through generations is held by many distinct civilizations and most likely dates back thousands of years.

I'm a great believer that we have to go back to the source at the very beginning to find the answers. And once we do it will all make perfect sense.

Let us look into the background of Transgenerational Trauma, and as we do we will begin to realise that it has been around for centuries and that we are only just touching the surface.

And how it is affecting the millions of people around the world who are suffering today from depression, anxiety, stress, fear; and the list goes on. It is an invisible disease that is causing so much unhappiness. And where do we get the help we so desperately need?

I am not saying I have all the answers, and I am not saying it is guaranteed; of course not. Doctors don't guarantee anything, either. But just suppose a percentage of those suffering can be helped through The Loveday Method. Would it be worth it?

I want to answer that question. The answers you are searching for are in this book.

Transgenerational Trauma is a fascinating and complex phenomenon that has far-reaching implications for individuals, families, and society as a whole. While the concept has only recently gained recognition in the Western world, it has been a part of many cultures for centuries, and the effects of generational trauma can be seen in communities around the world.

One of the most compelling aspects of Transgenerational Trauma is the way in which it is transmitted across generations. Trauma can be passed down through biological means, such as changes in DNA and the epigenome, as well as through cultural and societal means, such as storytelling and cultural practices. The effects of Transgenerational Trauma can be profound, influencing the mental and physical health of individuals, families, and even entire communities.

Moreover, research has shown that the consequences of Transgenerational Trauma can be particularly severe for the children of trauma survivors. Studies have linked the offspring of Holocaust survivors to higher rates of mental and physical health problems, providing compelling evidence for the intergenerational transmission of trauma.

As society becomes more aware of the impact of Transgenerational Trauma, there is growing interest in exploring the ways in which it can be treated and prevented. For example, interventions such as trauma-focused therapy and parenting support programs can help break the cycle of generational trauma, improving outcomes for both individuals and families.

Native North American tribes and Native Americans

It's important to remember that both Native North American tribes and Native Americans have unique histories, cultures, and experiences that have shaped who they are today. Despite their differences, both groups have faced significant challenges, including

Transgenerational Trauma, as a result of the violence and oppression they have endured throughout history. By recognizing and understanding these differences and similarities, we can work towards building a more inclusive and empathetic society that supports and uplifts all individuals, regardless of their background or ancestry.

As the sun sets over the vast expanse of the North American continent, a deep-seated sense of pain and trauma still lingers in the hearts and minds of many Native Americans. For centuries, they have been the victims of unspeakable violence and oppression at the hands of both their own indigenous groups and European settlers.

These experiences have left a lasting legacy of Transgenerational Trauma that is passed down from one generation to the next. Despite the passage of time, the wounds inflicted upon Native Americans still fester, leaving scars that run deep and wide.

But there is hope. In the traditions of many Native American tribes, there is a belief that their ancestors continue to guide and protect them, even after death.

Through dreams, symbols, and signs, their ancestors offer guidance and comfort, helping to ease the burden of the trauma that they carry.

However, the struggle for healing and reconciliation is far from over. Discrimination and racism against Native Americans continue to this day, making it difficult for them to feel safe and secure in their own land. But with the resilience and strength that has sustained them for centuries, they continue to fight for justice and equality.

Through the stories of their past and present, we can learn about the beauty and pain of Native American culture and gain a deeper understanding of the ongoing struggles they face. It is up to all of us to stand with them and work towards a brighter future, one that honours their rich heritage and recognizes the injustices of the past.

Chinese Culture

Are you ready to delve into the mysterious world of Chinese culture? Get ready to experience a belief that emotions can be passed down from one generation to the next, causing overwhelming physical and mental health problems. As you delve deeper into the fascinating beliefs of this ancient culture, you'll discover that the key to preventing these problems lies in releasing these emotions through the generations.

But wait, there's more! This belief isn't just rooted in myth and legend. Science has shown that trauma can actually cause changes in the brain that are passed down to future generations, meaning that negative emotions really can be inherited. Whether you're a skeptic or a believer, the impact of emotions on our lives is undeniable. They can influence our health, our relationships, and our overall well-being. So what are you waiting for? Embark on a journey through Chinese culture and discover the power of emotions.

African American.

Similarly, in African American communities, it is believed that the trauma of slavery and discrimination can be passed down through generations, leading to higher rates of chronic illnesses, such as diabetes and heart disease, as well as mental health issues like depression and anxiety.

Japanese Beliefs

There is a belief in Japan that emotions and experiences can be passed down from one generation to the next. This is known as the theory of "keishō sa reta keishitsu", or "inherited traits."

This theory suggests that our ancestors' memories and emotions are stored in our DNA and that we can access them through our subconscious. This means that we may be influenced by the things our ancestors experienced, even if we don't consciously remember them.

Some people believe that this explains why certain fears or phobias may be passed down through families. For example, a person who is afraid of heights may have an ancestor who died in a fall. The fear of heights would then be passed down through their DNA.

"Keishō sa reta keishitsu" is also thought to explain why some people are drawn to certain places or things. For example, someone may be drawn to a country because their ancestors lived there. Or, they may be attracted to a certain type of music because their ancestors enjoyed it.

There is no scientific evidence to support the theory. However, it is an interesting way to think about our connection to our ancestors and the things they experienced. It may also help us to understand our fears and attractions.

Do you think the theory of "keishō sa reta keishitsu" is plausible? What other cultures believe that the traumas of our ancestors are affecting our lives today and that we are living someone else's life and that the emotions we are living were there before we were born? Do you think this is possible?

It is believed that the events that occurred in our ancestors' lives can have an impact on our own lives. This is because it is thought that their memories and emotions are stored in our DNA. So, if they experienced something traumatic, we may be more likely to experience it as well.

The Aeta

The Aeta people's belief in Transgenerational Trauma runs deep, ingrained in their cultural heritage and shamanistic practices. They hold the firm belief that the experiences of their ancestors can impact their lives and the lives of future generations. This profound belief has shaped their worldview and has been a driving force in their efforts to heal from past traumas.

The Aeta's shamanistic practices are a testament to their resilience and their unwavering faith in the power of the human spirit to overcome adversity. Through their shamanistic rituals, the Aeta seek to connect with their ancestors and heal the wounds of the past. These rituals involve the use of medicinal plants, music, dance, and prayer, all of which are believed to have a powerful healing effect on the mind, body, and soul.

Despite the challenges facing the Aeta people, their steadfast belief in the power of their cultural heritage and the resilience of the human spirit continues to inspire people around the world. Their story is a testament to the strength and beauty of indigenous cultures and the importance of preserving these cultures for future generations.

Just suppose it is true that genetics are passed down from one generation to the next that it is affecting our lives today and that it was there before we were born that we are reliving the feelings and emotions of our ancestors.

So where do we find the answers?

"We design our lives through the power of choices."
Richard Bach

Chapter 21: The Loveday Method.

So where does The Loveday Method come in?

The Loveday Method is a sophisticated means of achieving time travel through the mind to access hidden memories within the DNA that are responsible for generational trauma.

Inherited Therapy is a new approach to helping people to release this invisible force that is controlling people's lives today.

Just suppose you could access a part of the brain and navigate through the mind to relive the feelings and emotions of our ancestors and experience what they felt and how their life's journey affects our life today and give them back.

To be able to take you on a journey where you will relive a moment in the first person as your grandfather, grandmother, uncles, and aunts and let go of the traumas you have been holding onto.

The answers you are searching for are hidden in this book. So let us take a look at the science behind it. And then you decide.

Transgenerational Trauma is a form of psychological trauma that is passed down from one generation to the next.

In medical literature, the first study concerning the transgenerational effects of trauma in OHS was published in 1966. The author, Dr Vivian Rakoff, was a researcher at the Jewish General Hospital in Montreal, a city where thousands of Holocaust survivors had settled.[5]

Dr Vivian Rakoff is a world-renowned expert on Transgenerational Trauma. She has worked with survivors of the Holocaust, as well as other groups who have suffered from genocide and mass violence.

In her work, Dr Rakoff has found that Transgenerational Trauma is a real and powerful force in the world. It is something that is passed down from

---

[5]https://www.ncbi.nlm.nih.gov/pmc/articles/PMC3500267/#:~:text=In%20the%20medical%20literature%2C%20the,survivors%20had%20settled%20%5B4%5D.

one generation to the next, and it can have a profound impact on the lives of those who suffer from it.

This can lead to several different problems for those who suffer from it. Fortunately, there is help available for those who suffer from Transgenerational Trauma. Several different therapy options can be used to help people heal from the trauma that they have experienced.

Has there been any research that children can be affected by the emotions of our ancestors which is affecting their lives today?

Yes, there is research on whether children can inherit the fears and illnesses that were present in their parents or grandparents before they were born. This is called "Transgenerational Trauma."

Transgenerational Trauma can be caused by things like war, natural disasters, genocide, and sexual abuse. This can lead to several mental and physical health problems, including Post Traumatic Stress Disorder (PTSD), anxiety, depression, substance abuse, and even physical health problems.

It can also affect a person's ability to form healthy relationships and make good decisions. If you think you may be suffering from Transgenerational Trauma, it is important to seek professional help. Several treatments can help you heal from this type of trauma.

One study on Transgenerational Trauma was conducted by Rachel Yehuda, a professor of psychiatry at the Icahn School of Medicine at Mount Sinai in New York. The study was published in the Journal of Clinical Psychiatry in 2001.

The study found that children of Holocaust survivors were more likely to suffer from PTSD, anxiety, and depression than children of those who has not suffered in the Holocaust. The study also found that the grandchildren of Holocaust survivors were also more likely to have symptoms of PTSD.

Another study, which was published in Biological Psychiatry in 2015 found that Holocaust survivors who developed post-traumatic stress disorder (PTSD) were more likely to have grandchildren with PTSD than those who did not develop the disorder.[6]

The two studies were different in that the second study specifically looked at the effects of Transgenerational Trauma on children of Holocaust survivors

This study is important because it suggests that trauma can be passed down from one generation to the next. This has major implications for our understanding of mental health and how we treat it.

A further study on Transgenerational Trauma was conducted by Elaine Miller, a professor of psychology at the University of New Hampshire. The study was published in the Journal of Traumatic Stress in 2006.

The study found that children of parents who were exposed to the 9–11 attacks were more likely to have symptoms of PTSD than children whose parents were not exposed to the attacks.

---

[6] Yehuda, R., & LeDoux, J. (2001). The neurobiology of fear conditioning: Implications for posttraumatic stress disorder. Journal of Clinical Psychiatry, 62(Suppl 3), 22-31.

Her research focused on the effects of exposure to violence and trauma on children's developing sense of self. She found that children who were exposed to violence and trauma were more likely to have a negative view of themselves and the world around them. These children were also more likely to have difficulty regulating their emotions and were more likely to engage in risky behaviours.[7]

Miller's research highlights the importance of providing support to children who have been exposed to violence and trauma. These children must receive counselling and other forms of support to help them heal from their experiences.

Additionally, it is important for adults who work with these children to be aware of the potential effects of exposure to violence and trauma. By understanding the impact of these experiences, adults can provide the necessary support to help children heal and thrive.

These two studies are just a snapshot of the research that has been conducted on Transgenerational Trauma. There is still much more to

---

[7] Miller, E. K., & Rasmussen, A. (2006). Transgenerational effects of the September 11th terrorist attacks. Journal of Traumatic Stress, 19(5), 727-736.

learn about this topic. However, the studies that have been conducted so far suggest that children can indeed inherit the fears and illnesses of their parents or grandparents. Many treatments can help you heal from this type of trauma.

"Whether you think you can or you think you can't, you're right."
Henry Ford

PART THREE

Chapter 22: An Unseen Influence

An unseen influence. An unknown driving force. Where did it originate from? What gives us this impression, and why? And could we be focusing our efforts in the wrong place to find the answers?

Imagine for a moment that these emotions that are causing us to experience such a great deal of unhappiness did not originate from within ourselves. They were bequeathed to us by previous generations of our family. Something that happened much later in life prompted these feelings in each of us.

We are living the lives of our ancestors, and the adversities that they faced in their lives are having an effect on our lives in the present day. Now we are starting to get a better understanding of where it came from. Therefore, what should we do next? What are the next steps after this?

Now we're getting to the part where things start to become interesting. Imagine for a moment that you could go through time, live the life of one of your ancestors, impart upon them the emotion that you are clinging to, and solve the fundamental issue at hand. It is possible that by doing this, you would be able to change the course of their life, and subsequently the course of your own.

If we can go back and change the emotions of our ancestors, then we can change our future. We can break the cycle that has been passed down to us, and forge our path. This is an interesting proposition and one worth further exploration.

Now let us look deeper into this concept of going back in time to change the emotions of our ancestors. It is important to first understand the mechanics of how this could be possible. Once we have a good understanding of the how we can then start to think about the why.

The act of going back in time and changing the emotions of our ancestors is not something that can be done with our current understanding of physics. To do this, we would need to find a way to bend or break the laws of physics. This is admittedly a tall order, but not an impossible one. There have been many advances in physics over the past few decades, and who knows what the future holds? It is not outside the realm of possibility that we may one day find a way to bend or break the laws of physics, and if we do, then we would be able to go back in time and change the emotions of our ancestors. If time lets us.

Even if we are unable to find a way to bend or break the laws of physics, there is still hope. We may not be able to travel back in time and change the emotions of our ancestors, but we can still change our own emotions. We can choose to let go of the emotions that are causing us pain and instead focus on the positive aspects of our lives.

This may not seem like much, but it is a start. And who knows? Maybe, just maybe, if we all start to focus on the positive aspects of our lives, we can create a ripple effect that will change the emotions of our ancestors, and ultimately change the course of our future.

It is important to remember that we are not alone in this. We are part of a larger whole, and everything that we do affects the whole. We may not be able to see it, but our actions impact those around us, those around them, and so on. It is important to be mindful of the ripple effect that our actions can have and to try to always act in a way that will create a positive ripple effect.

So, the next time you find you are feeling unhappy or stuck in a cycle of negative emotions, take a moment to think about where those emotions might have come from. They were possibly passed down to you from your ancestors. If this is the case, then know that you have the power to break the cycle. You can choose to let go of those negative emotions, and instead focus on the positive. It may not seem like much, but it is a start. And who knows? Maybe, just maybe, if we all start to focus on the positive, we can create a ripple effect that will change the course of our future.

Imagine for a moment that you had access to a portion of the brain and the ability to go through the mind to relive the sensations and emotions of our ancestors and experience what they felt and how their life's journey affects our lives today and gives them back.

Let me assure you that there is a solution available to you in the form of The Loveday Method. By using The Loveday Method, you can mentally travel back in time to retrieve the traumatic experiences that have been passed down from generation to generation and free yourself from the grip that trauma has had on your family for generations. And in this book lies the key to that Method.

Energy and how it affects our lives

It never ceases to amaze me how our actions may have an unintended impact on the emotions of those around us, how trivial disagreements can quickly become heated and cause pain for both parties involved, and how difficult it can be for us to let go of what we are experiencing on the inside.

The humble expression of regret in the form of "I'm sorry" can have a significant weight. Is it your ignorance or your obstinacy that holds you back? But when you consider all that took place, do you think it was that significant? Does it even make a difference? Both the things that we say and the deeds that we carry out require caution on our part. What we choose to do with our lives has a significant effect on the people we care about.

Now let us first talk about energy to give you an understanding of who we are. What do we see when we examine the human body? Looking inside the human body, we find a complex system of organs and tissues that work together to keep us alive. But what exactly is going on inside our bodies? Is energy involved as well as matter?

It turns out that the answer is a bit of both. Our bodies are made up of atoms, which are particles of matter. But these atoms are constantly in motion, and they also have energy. This energy is what keeps our bodies going.

In addition to the energy from atoms, our bodies also need other forms of energy to function properly. For example, we need sunlight to produce vitamin D, and we need food to provide us with the calories we need to live. So, while our bodies are made up of matter, they also rely on energy to function. This energy comes from a variety of sources, both inside and outside our bodies.

Messages from Water

"Messages from Water: The World's First Water Crystal Photo-book"

by Masaru Emoto

I am sure that many of you have seen the beautiful pictures of water crystals that Dr Masaru Emoto[8] has taken. These pictures show how words and thoughts can change the structure of water. The implications of this research are vast, and I believe that the findings can help us to understand the true nature of reality.

In his book, The Hidden Messages in Water, Dr Emoto shares his findings and provides readers with an in-depth look at the amazing properties of water.

[8] https://en.wikipedia.org/wiki/Masaru_Emoto

He also offers insights into the power of words and thoughts, and how they can impact our lives and the world around us.

This book is a must-read for anyone interested in learning more about the true nature of reality. It is an eye–opening and thought–provoking look at the power of words and thoughts, and how they can impact our lives and the world around us.

Did you know that water has a memory? It's true! Water can remember a thing that has happened to it in the past.

This was discovered by Dr Masaru Emoto, a Japanese scientist who has been studying water for many years. He has found that water molecules change when they are exposed to different energies.

For example, water that has been exposed to positive energy – like kind words or beautiful music – will have lovely, symmetrical crystals when it is frozen.

On the other hand, water that has been exposed to negative energy – like ugly words or scary music – will have jagged and uneven crystals.

This shows that water is deeply affected by the energies around it. And since we are made mostly of water, this means that we are too!

So what does this have to do with Messages From Water? Well, Dr Emoto has found that water can actually "remember" certain messages – even if they're written down on a piece of paper!

He did an experiment where he wrote different messages on pieces of paper and then taped them to bottles of water which were taken from different reservoirs and lakes. After a few days, he froze the water and looked at the crystals under a microscope. The results were amazing! The water that had been exposed to positive messages had beautiful crystals, while the water that had been exposed to negative messages had uneven and jagged crystals.

So what does this mean for us? Well, it means that we should be careful about the kind of energy and vibrations we expose ourselves to.

If we want to have beautiful, healthy bodies and minds, we should surround ourselves with positive energy as much as possible. We can do this by listening to uplifting music, spending time in nature, being around positive people, and so on.

On the other hand, we should try to avoid negative energy as much as possible. This includes things like watching too much news, listening to angry music and spending time with negative people.

Of course, we can't avoid all negative energy – it's a part of life. But the more positive energy we surround ourselves with, the more it will help offset the negative.

So next time you're feeling down, try exposing yourself to some positive energy – it might just help you feel better!

Experiments with Rice and Water

Dr Masaru Emoto

Please take the time to watch the video that this link leads to. You will be amazed at the results.

https://youtu.be/Ehlw-9PJkIE

Dr Masaru Emoto is a Japanese doctor who has conducted extensive research on the effects of human thoughts and emotions on water. His experiments have shown that positive thoughts and emotions can change the structure of water, making it more beautiful and harmonious, while negative thoughts and emotions can make water more chaotic and ugly.

One of Dr Emoto's most famous experiments is the "rice experiment." In this experiment, Dr Emoto took three jars of rice and added water to them. He then labelled one jar "Thank you", the second "You idiot", and the third "Neglected". Every day for 30 days, he would say the respective labels out loud to each jar of rice ignoring the neglected jar.

At the end of the 30 days, the rice in the "Thank you" jar was still fresh, while the rice in the "You fool" jar had turned rotten, and the rice in the neglected jar had gone mouldy. This experiment demonstrates the power of human thoughts and emotions on water.

Dr Emoto's research has shown that positive thoughts and emotions can have a profound effect on the quality of water, and by extension, the quality of our lives. If you're interested in learning more about Dr Masaru Emoto's work, I highly recommend checking out his books: The Hidden Messages in Water; and The Secret Life of Water. As someone who is fascinated by the power of human thoughts and emotions, I was intrigued by this experiment. It's amazing to think that such simple things as our thoughts and emotions can have such a profound effect on the world around us.

If you're interested in learning more about the power of your thoughts and emotions, I highly recommend checking out "The Secret" by Rhonda Byrne. This book is all about the power of positive thinking and how it can change your life for the better.

Adam Mock

https://www.adammock.com

Adam Mock's rice and water experiment lasted for two years. He labelled one jar Love, the second jar Hate, and the third jar Neutral.

Watch his YouTube channel and see what happened. Notice how Adam puts feelings and beliefs when he talks to the jars. This is so important.

You can watch the experiments here:

https://www.youtube.com/watch?v=r_h8jWlyYBs or https://youtu.be/r_h8jWlyYBs.

This is the interview I did with Adam. (Click the link below)

https://www.inheritedtherapy.com

Geoffrey Loveday

After watching all of these, I decided to experiment myself for 42 days, as I like to test my work. But my test will be a little different I will use six jars; three jars with lids, and three without lids. And the tests ran for 42 days and 63 days instead of just 30 days.

Each jar will be separate from the others. We will go through each day and see what happens.

Test one:

As you can see, the three glass jars have no lids.

Day 1: Tuesday 25th October 2022.
The first bottle is labelled:	"LOVE"
The second bottle is labelled:	"HATE"
The third bottle is labelled:	"IGNORED"

Equal amounts of cooked rice and water were added, just five tablespoons of the same cooked rice in each jar.

Neglect Jar:

The rice in the Neglect jar started turning yellow after 12 days.

After 42 days, the Neglect jar was well on its way to rotting completely.

Hate Jar:

After eight days, the Hate jar started to show signs of mould. And by day 12, the mould was spreading.

After 42 days, the Hate jar is also decomposing, worse than the Neglect jar, and is rotting faster.

Love Jar:

After the first eight days, the Love jar showed no signs of mould or yellowing.

After twelve days, the Love jar was still in good form and showed no signs of rot. And after a full 42 days, it had merely dried up from water evaporation at room temperature, and still showed no sign of decomposition.

I would always leave the jars in a cupboard, away from light and direct heat. I'd only take them out one at a time to interact with them, leaving the neglect jar in the cupboard.

The 42-day test reveals some incredible results, both in terms of how it affects rice and how it changes the water around it just by having a conversation with them.

- Neglect Jar: Rice rotting
- Hate Jar: Rice rotting
- Love Jar: No change looks a bit dry.

Test 2:

As you can see, the three glass jars all have lids.

Day 1: Tuesday 25th October 2022.
The first bottle is labelled: "LOVE"
The second bottle is labelled: "HATE"
The third bottle is labelled: "IGNORED"

Equal amounts of cooked rice and water were added, just five tablespoons of the same cooked rice in each jar.

After 63 days, this is the result of the experiment.

Neglect Jar: Day 63

Hate Jar: Day 63

Love Jar: Day 63

If you look closely at the images above, you'll note that although the Love jar test done with lids is still wet, the love jar without a lid is quite dry. Is this because it was safe from the outside world when the lids were on?

I also noticed the smell of the three jars was different. The scent of both of the love jars was sweet, while the others were not so nice.

Now replace the Rice and water experiment with three children

Consider the experiment with the rice and the water. You will treat one child with love, the other with hatred and humiliation, and the third child throughout that child's entire life you will ignore altogether.

What kind of an impact will it have on those three children's lives in the years to come? What do you think will happen to them in the future?

So what have we learned?

If just words written on paper have such an effect on rice and water, how do negative emotions affect the human body?

Negative emotions have been shown to have a profound effect on the human body. They can negatively impact our immune system, our cardiovascular system, and our nervous system.

They can also lead to inflammation and an increased risk of disease. So it's important to be aware of the power of our thoughts and emotions and to try to keep them positive as much as possible.

The Power of Plants

In general, plants have a positive effect on the power of words. This is because plants produce oxygen, which is necessary for human beings to live. Oxygen helps to increase the clarity of thoughts and ideas and also aids in memory retention. Furthermore, plants help to purify the air, making it easier for people to breathe. Thus, by their presence, plants can help to make the power of words more potent.

Do plants hold water?

The answer is yes, plants do hold water. This is because plants are composed of cells, and these cells contain a vacuole. A vacuole is a type of cell organelle that stores water. When a plant cell is full of water, it is said to be turgid. Turgidity is important for the plant cell because it helps the plant cell to maintain its shape. If a plant cell loses too much water, it will become flaccid and may even collapse.

What percentage of water does a plant hold?

There is no definitive answer to this question as it depends on the plant species and the conditions under which the plant is growing. However, it is generally accepted that most plants hold between 50% and 90% water by weight. Consequently, a plant that weighs 100 grams (3.5 ounces) would likely contain between 50 and 90 grams of water.

How does water get into the plant?

Water enters the plant through the roots. The roots are typically buried in the soil, and as the plant absorbs water from the soil, the water is drawn up through the roots and into the plant. Once inside the plant, the water travels through the xylem tissue. The xylem is a type of tissue that consists of tubes that transport water and nutrients throughout the plant.

Can talking to plants affect them?

There is no scientific evidence to support the claim that talking to plants has any effect. However, some people believe that talking to plants helps them to grow better. This may be because the act of talking to plants gives the person a sense of connection with the plant, and this feeling of connection can help to promote growth. Additionally, some people believe that the vibrations produced by talking can help to stimulate plant growth. While there is no scientific evidence to support these claims, they are nonetheless held by some people.

Because they are sensitive to vibrations, the question arises as to whether or not talking to plants genuinely encourages their growth.

We all know that plants need water, sunlight, and love to grow. But what about talking to them? Does that make a difference?

It turns out that plants may not be as good at listening as we are, but they can still respond to the vibrations of our voices. Studies have shown that plants can change their growth patterns when they are spoken to.

So, does this mean that we should all start talking to our plants?

It couldn't hurt! At the very least, it might make them feel appreciated. And who knows, maybe they'll even grow a little bit taller.

The Placebo Effect

What is the placebo effect?

The placebo effect is the phenomenon whereby a given treatment, procedure or medication produces a therapeutic effect in a patient, even though it is not medically effective. Placebo effects can occur in both positive and negative ways – that is, a placebo can sometimes improve a patient's condition, while at other times it may worsen it. Either way, the effect is due to the patient's beliefs and expectations about the treatment, rather than to any actual physical or chemical properties of the treatment itself.

There are many examples of the placebo effect in action. For instance, patients who believe that they are receiving a powerful new pain medication may indeed experience relief from their pain, even if the medication is an inert placebo.

Similarly, patients who are told that a certain medical procedure will be painful may indeed find it so, even if the procedure is quite painless.

The placebo effect is thought to work by activating the body's natural healing mechanisms. When we believe that we are receiving a helpful treatment, our bodies respond accordingly, releasing hormones and chemicals that promote healing. This positive response can sometimes be enough to offset the effects of a real medical condition.

Interestingly, the placebo effect is not just confined to medicine. Placebo effects have been documented in all sorts of different contexts, from sports performance to economic decision-making. In each case, it seems that our beliefs and expectations can exert a powerful influence on our behaviour and outcomes.

Hope, belief and most importantly love. How can a placebo influence our thoughts?

A little boy, around 7 years old, is experiencing nightmares. As you might understand, the child does not want to sleep. His father informs the youngster about a new liquid that has been produced over the previous 10 years and is guaranteed to end nightmares.[9]

He says he'll call the doctor to check if he has any of this medicine in stock because it's so new that he might not have any. He tells the youngster it's extremely bitter and that it's normally only for adults, and he's not sure whether he should take it.

The youngster is quite anxious to give this a try. The father attempts to talk him out of it but eventually agrees. He then takes the youngster downstairs while pretending to contact the doctor.

---

[9] A similar story is taken from the book, Hypnotherapy, by Dave Elman, on pages 67 and 68.

He tells the child that he needs to be a courageous young child to take it, but he knows he is brave, and the doctor will send it over. While he is speaking to the doctor on the phone, his mother locates a tiny, empty bottle, fills it with water, and labels it.

To ensure the youngster listens, his father pretends there is a knock at the door. Even though it's intended for adults, he walks upstairs and asks the youngster whether he is sure he wants to consume something so unpleasant.

I'm sure, the youngster responds.

Hold your nose because it is so bitter, that's fantastic, his father said. The child says it tastes awful. Every night after taking his medication, the youngster enjoyed the most incredible sleep, sleeping like a baby.

It's amazing how giving hope belief and love has such an effect on that child.

So next time you're feeling under the weather, remember that the power of positive thinking just might be enough to make you feel better!

Read this amazing story about a child and her mother. This is truly magic.

"I was talking to Geof recently about my daughter and the nightmare we had at her birth. When Grace was born, the Doctor who delivered her damaged her arm resulting in an Erb's Palsy injury and he dislocated both of her hips.

"Concerning her hips, we were told at our initial consultation at the hospital that she would only have a 6% chance of full recovery due to how badly the hips were damaged; in particular the left one was really bad. I remember saying at the time, after the tears had stopped, "no this isn't Grace's reality, this isn't what is meant to happen and she is going to recover I will make sure of it".

"Every day I would research ways to help her, I was so determined and I would tell her every day that she was getting better. Every week that passed I felt like we were getting there. I researched ways to hold her (as she was in a full-body harness), I researched ways to help her hip position and I kept telling her she would get through this.

"I wouldn't allow any negative talk about her situation and I wouldn't allow anyone to tell me that she was going to be anything other than ok. My mind was so focused on the fact she would be fine. I kept telling myself it over and over again, even when I slept, I was dreaming about her getting better. I was dreaming about holding her without her harness on and I was focused on the positive.

"We attended appointments every 2 weeks for monitoring and to the Doctor's astonishment, each appointment showed that Grace was healing. We finally got to our last appointment when Grace was 5 and half months old and the Doctor said to me "it is a miracle, her hips are perfect". After 5 and a half long, hard months, we got the result I knew we would from day one. She had perfect hips and that horrible harness was gone for good.

"Given the fact we were told at the first appointment even though she would be wearing the harness, the likelihood was that she would need surgery and to be put in a spica cast to then be told that it wasn't needed as her hips were perfect was just the most amazing feeling. It was tears of joy this time, not of sorrow. We were released from the Pavlik harness early, Grace originally was meant to wear it for 6 months but we managed to get ahead of schedule and Grace was free of it half a month earlier than planned.

"Looking back, I can see how determined I was. My life completely stopped and I even stopped communicating with most people because my life at that point was solely focused on getting Grace to where she needed to be. I am so proud of her. She handled it without any issues. The power of positivity is amazing."

Kirlian Photography

Kirlian Photography is a technique used to photograph the electrical fields around objects. It is named after Semyon Kirlian, who discovered the effect in 1939.

Kirlian Photography has been used to study the aura, or energy field, around people and objects. The technique is controversial, as there is no scientific evidence that the aura exists. However, many people believe that the aura is real and that it can be seen in Kirlian photographs.

Kirlian Photography is not a true photography technique, as it does not use film or a digital sensor. Instead, it uses a high-voltage electrical field to ionise the air around an object. This creates a glow which can be photographed.

Kirlian Photography is used by some alternative healers to diagnose illness. It is also used by some psychics to see a person's aura.

Critics of Kirlian Photography say that the technique is not scientific and that the aura does not exist. They also say that the photographs can be faked, as the electrical field can be created without an object being present. Kirlian Photography is also criticised for its lack of reproducibility, as different photographers get different results.

Despite the criticism, Kirlian Photography remains popular and is used by many people who believe in the existence of the aura.

The Power of Belief

Faith's transformative potential.

The life of Roger Bannister serves as an excellent example. Roger Banister broke the four-minute mile barrier, becoming the first person to do so. Because he put in the time at the gym and trusted in his abilities, he was able to achieve his goal. To everyone's amazement, he managed to run a mile in under four minutes, proving that with enough dedication and confidence, one can achieve almost anything. People can be motivated to greatness by hearing this message.

If you have faith in yourself and are prepared to put in the effort, you can do anything. This is the lesson we can learn from Roger Banister's life. It's an uplifting story about how much one man can achieve with a can–do mentality and a little bit of luck. The only way to fail is to limit yourself to the level of success you think is achievable.

But if you have faith in yourself and are prepared to put in the effort, nothing will stand in your way. Imagine the best for yourself and never stop believing in your ability to achieve your goals. You can make them come true through persistent effort and faith in yourself.

Was it simply the time he spent in the gym and his confidence in his ability to run a mile in under four minutes?

Or was it something magical?

Was his belief so strong he changed the frequency in his body with the power of thoughts and words that he told himself?

It makes you think, but I suppose we will never know.

The Power of the Mind

The human mind is incredibly complex, and there are many unseen influences at work. One of the most powerful influences is the subconscious mind.

The subconscious mind is responsible for our automatic behaviours and reactions. It also stores all of our memories, both good and bad. Our beliefs and values are also stored in the subconscious mind.

The subconscious mind is a very powerful force. It can influence our thoughts, feelings, and behaviours in ways that we are not even aware of. It is important to be aware of the power of the subconscious mind so that we can make sure that we are living our lives in a way that is in alignment with our deepest desires and values.

Is the human mind a computer?

The idea that the human mind is a computer has been around for centuries and has been proposed by many different thinkers. The most famous proponent of this view is probably the philosopher René

Descartes,[10] who argued that the mind is like a machine that can be programmed to perform certain tasks.

More recently, the cognitive scientist Marvin Minsky[11] has argued that the mind is a type of computer and that human beings can perform complex tasks because they have access to a vast amount of information that is stored in their brains.

In thinking about the significance of his work, it is clear that Dr Minsky has made many contributions to artificial intelligence, cognitive psychology, mathematics, computational linguistics, robotics, and optics. In recent years, he has worked chiefly on imparting to machines the human capacity for common sense reasoning.

Critics of the view that the mind is a computer argue that this analogy does not accurately capture the way that the mind works. They point out that computers are designed to perform specific tasks, and

---

[10] https://plato.stanford.edu/entries/descartes/
[11] https://www.fi.edu/laureates/marvin-minsky

they cannot switch to performing other tasks without being programmed to do so.

In contrast, the human mind is much more flexible and can adapt to new situations and learn new skills relatively easily. Additionally, critics argue that the view of the mind as a computer fails to explain why humans have consciousness, whereas computers do not.

Despite the criticisms of the view that the mind is a computer, it remains a popular analogy and one that has some plausibility. After all, computers can perform complex tasks, and they can store vast amounts of information.

Additionally, recent advances in artificial intelligence have shown that computers can be programmed to perform some tasks that were previously thought to require consciousness, such as recognizing faces or understanding natural language. However, it is important to remember that the mind is a very complex system and that the analogy between the mind and a computer is far from perfect.

Now let us bring the past into the present.

Émile Coué

Émile Coué[12] was a French psychologist and pharmacist who developed the "Law of Reversed Effort", which states that one can achieve their goals more easily by focusing on what one wants to achieve, rather than on what one does not want. Coué's methods were based on his belief that the mind could heal the body, and he used autosuggestion to help his patients overcome their illnesses.

---

[12] https://en.wikipedia.org/wiki/%C3%89mile_Cou%C3%A9

Coué was born in Troyes, France, on February 26, 1857. He studied pharmacy at the University of Paris and graduated in 1881. After working as a pharmacist for several years, Coué began to study psychology, and he soon developed an interest in hypnosis. He began to use hypnosis to help his patients, and he found that it was an effective way to treat various illnesses. In 1904, Coué opened a clinic in Nancy, France, where he treated patients using his methods of autosuggestion.

Coué's method of autosuggestion involved having his patients repeat positive affirmations to themselves. He believed that by doing this, his patients could change their negative thoughts and beliefs into positive ones, which would then lead to improved health. Coué's work was based on the idea that the mind can heal the body, and he believed that his methods could help people to overcome a wide range of ailments.

What autosuggestion was he most famous for? Almost everyone may have heard of this:

"Every day and in every way I'm getting better and better."

The Coué method is a psychological self-help technique that was developed by French psychologist Émile Coué in the early 20th century. The method involves repeating a positive affirmation to oneself multiple times per day to change one's mind-set and improve one's outlook on life.

The affirmations are typically specific, personal, and present tense, such as "I am healthy and happy." The technique is based on the theory that our thoughts influence our actions and emotions, and by repeating positive affirmations we can program our minds to think more positively, resulting in improved health and happiness.

The Coué method was first popularised in the 1920s and experienced a resurgence in popularity in the 1960s and 1970s. Today, the technique is used by people all over the world as a way to improve their mental and physical health. While there is no scientific evidence to support the efficacy of the Coué method, many people report positive results from using it.

If you're interested in trying the Coué method, there are a few things you should keep in mind.

First, it's important to choose affirmations that are specific and personal to you. Second, the affirmations should be said out loud, multiple times per day. And finally, it's important to believe in the power of affirmations to see results.

If you're looking for a way to improve your health and happiness, the Coué method may be worth a try. Who knows, it might just work for you!

Coué's work did fall out of favour in the 1930s when behaviourism became the dominant school of thought in psychology. However, his ideas were revived in the 1950s by Albert Ellis, who developed a form of cognitive–behavioural therapy known as rational–emotive therapy.

Coué died on July 2, 1926, in Nancy, France. Although his work was largely forgotten after his death, his work and credit have been revived in recent years by psychologists who are interested in the power of positive thinking.

Putting the Pieces Together

You must see that a puzzle is taking shape and that as we put the pieces together, we realise that the things we say over and over to ourselves and the people we care about have profound effects on us and them.

Now, let's take a closer look to see how it affects our children and future generations of our children.

As water may be altered by vibrations alone, an unseen force is also capable of influencing our children.

Consider for a moment how our actions impact our children's lives. From an early period to the age of seven, your child absorbs information like a sponge. As parents, we must be careful of what we say and do. What you do today will affect your children as they grow up. Remember we are 74% water.

According to Mitchell and others, the average human being is composed of 74% water. Infants and children also average 74% water. The bones consist of

31% water, 64% is in the muscles, and the kidneys are 79% water. The heart is around 73% water, and the lungs are about 83%, which is much higher.

We must consume water each day to survive. Some say the human brain is 80% to 85% water. That's right, three–quarters of a brain is water, and even slight dehydration can cause fatigue headaches, lack of mental clarity, stress, and sleep issues. To hydrate the brain, women must consume between 2 and 2.7 litres of water a day, and men 2.5 to 3.7 litres, depending on several factors including activity, medication, and weight.

Now let us put the pieces together.

Dr Masaru Emoto experiments with rice and water. How written words and music affects water. Remember our brain is 80% to 85% water.

Émile Coué brings us auto–suggestion. Then we have the placebo effect, plants and how they respond to vibrations in our voice, and Roger Bannister and the power of belief.

Imagine for a moment that we could bring about the changes we seek by talking to ourselves about them over one month while maintaining a firm belief that this will work. What kinds of miracles might we expect to take place?

You can see how it changed the frequency of the water through positive words and thoughts. Don't forget we are 74% water and our brain is between 80% and 85% water. So let us work on the human mind.

And I dare you to take up this challenge.

PART FOUR

Chapter 23: The Thirty-Day Challenge

Firstly write down on a card or piece of paper exactly what you desire.

Keep it with you every second of the day even when you sleep at night.

You will repeat what it is you desire 30 times during the day.

<u>DO NOT</u> just say it, really believe it, see it, feel it.

Do this for 30 days, without missing a day.

Our thoughts are powerful because they create our reality. Everything starts with a thought, and as long as we believe in our thoughts, we can create the life we want.

Working on one thing at a time.

Chapter 24: Sleep Hypnosis

Hypnopaedia

Reprogramming our minds when we sleep.

Hypnopaedia is a method of sleep learning, which involves playing recorded messages or affirmations while a person is asleep. This technique is designed to help the individual learn new information or improve certain skills while they are in a state of rest. Some people believe that hypnopaedia can be an effective way to increase knowledge and improve performance in certain areas, although there is limited scientific evidence to support these claims. Additionally, it is important to note that hypnopaedia should only be used under the guidance of a qualified professional. Otherwise, there is a risk that the individual could experience negative side effects, such as sleep disruptions or anxiety.

Is Hypnopaedia dangerous? There is no evidence that hypnopaedia is dangerous. It may even be beneficial for some people.

The idea behind this was that the subconscious mind picks up on new information while we are sleeping and can help us learn new things more easily. This became known as hypnopaedia.

However, it is important to remember that it should not be used as a replacement for traditional methods of learning. It should be used in addition to these methods, as it can help to speed up the learning process and make it easier to retain information.

If you are interested in using hypnopaedia to learn something new, there are a few things you should keep in mind.

First, make sure that the recording you use is high quality and clear. The better the quality of the recording, the more likely it is that the subconscious will pick up on the information.

Second, it is important to find a comfortable place to listen to the recording. You should not listen to it while you are driving or doing other activities that could distract you. It is also important to make sure that you are in a relaxed state when you listen to the recording, as this will help your subconscious mind to better absorb the information.

Finally, it is important to have realistic expectations about what hypnopaedia can do for you. It is not a magic pill that will make you smarter or more skilled overnight. However, it can be a useful tool to help you learn new information more easily and retain it better.

If you are looking for a way to improve your memory, increase your intelligence, or learn new skills, hypnopaedia may be worth considering.

Sleep Hypnosis: Dave Elman

What is sleep hypnosis? Hypnosis attached to sleep: Hypno–sleep

Let me just mention Dave Elman. I feel that he has not been given the credit he deserves for his achievement in hypnosis; he was truly an amazing hypnotist and a pioneer in hypnosis.

This is a passage taken from the book, Hypnotherapy, by Dave Elman.[13] I feel it is only right that this passage you are about to read the credit should be given to an astounding hypnotist Dave Elman.

A man approached Mr Elman asked if he could speak to him privately, and said "Is it true that you teach your doctors how to hypnotise patients while they are fast asleep?"

"Yes," replied Elman

"I have to find a way to achieve this," said the man, "It is really important."

"Why is it so important?" asked Elman

"Mr Elman, my wife and I have been married for more than 35 years, and I hope that the future holds many more happy years for us. Throughout our marriage, I have had to deal with a terrible problem. In reality, my wife is the issue. However, I have a problem that has to be fixed. She always picks on me. You might refer to me as a henpecked husband."

---

[13] Hypnotherapy by Dave Elman: Book Chapter 22 Page 274. Hypnosis Attached To Sleep. Sleep Hypnosis.

"So, what's your plan?"

"Just this. She won't consent to be hypnotised. She won't even be aware that she's been hypnotised if I can do it while she is sound asleep. I can then make the required suggestions, and I'm confident that she will stop picking on me."

Mr Elman asked him not to enrol if this was his primary motivation for taking the course.

"Okay, Mr Elman," replied the man. "You undoubtedly have more knowledge on the subject than I do. I suppose I did get the wrong idea. Nevertheless, I'm going to sign up for the course because I think it would be beneficial for me to learn your methods so I may use them with my patients."

A year later he came to one of Elman's classes in the same city. He requested if he might address everyone, and Elman gave him the go-ahead.

You can hardly imagine the shock as he got up and said what follows.

"I had one goal in mind when I signed up to be Mr Elman's pupil. I wanted to learn how to hypnotise my wife while she was sleeping and give her advice to get her to quit picking on me."

"Mr Elman claimed that I couldn't do it and wouldn't succeed. However, I've achieved much more than success. Since my wife hasn't henpecked me in over a year, I can honestly claim that I've never been happier."

Isn't that amazing? Now just suppose we could use this technique on our children, while our children are fast asleep. So carry on reading.

Dave Elman employed this method on his son, who suffered from asthma at an early age also his allergy reactions grew worse as he got older.

He entered his son's room softly after he fell asleep. He said this, to be exact:

'You can hear me, but you won't wake up. You can hear me, but you won't wake up. When I touch your *little finger, I'll know you're listening when the finger moves. You can hear me, but you won't wake up,"* he said again. *"When this little finger starts moving, I'll know you're listening. You can move it, but you won't wake up."*

Gently, very slowly, he started to move his little finger. Elman was aware that the child could hear him and that he had hypnotised him while he was soundly asleep.

"I'm going to stop talking now and you'll fall fast asleep," he said before some suggestions were given. He then said, *"In the morning when you wake up, you won't even remember that I talked to you while you were asleep. You won't recall anything at all. We'll try this again tomorrow night, and I know you'll be open to it."*

He left the room as quietly as possible.

Conclusion?

When the Doctors asked him what good had been accomplished, he was able to inform them the outcomes have been quite remarkable. The allergic reactions were milder, and the bouts became less frequent.

So how does this help our children?

Whatever your child is suffering from, when your little one is fast asleep in bed, quietly go into the room and repeat this:

"This is your daddy (or mummy) speaking, you can hear me but you won't wake up. This is your daddy speaking, you can hear me but you won't wake up. You can hear me but you won't wake up . . . You can hear me but you won't wake up . . . You won't wake up . . . I'll know you're hearing me when the little finger that I'm touching begins to move."

Touch the finger gently, speak quietly and be persistent.

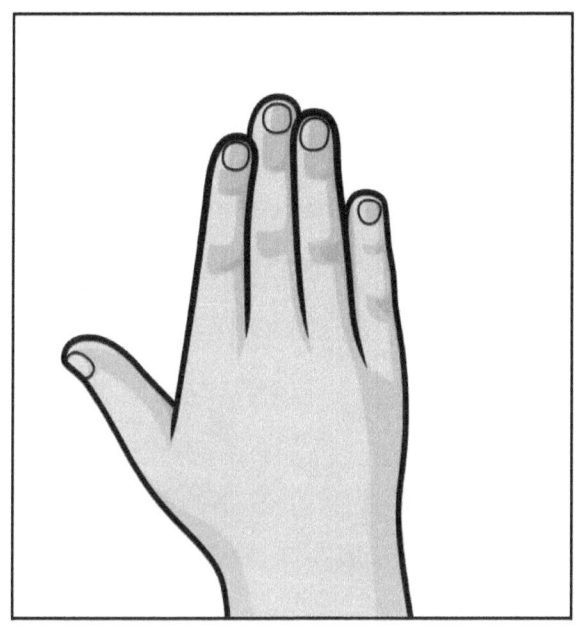

Once the finger moves he or she can hear you and they are open to suggestions.

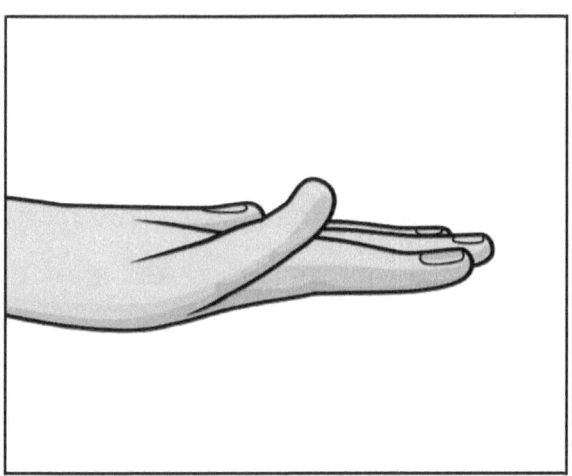

Example: For instance, let's assume the child is repeatedly naughty.

You will say "you are a good boy, your mummy loves you, your daddy loves you, and you love your mummy and daddy". Give only positive suggestions and repetition.

Repeat the suggestion for about one and a half minutes, no matter what the problem is.

This can help with biting nails, bedwetting, insomnia, being naughty, fear, and much more.

The finger has to move, as this will give you an indication that the child is listening and can hear you while asleep and respond to the suggestion given. And remember to be gentle, and try not to wake them up, but if you do, it's not a problem pretend to tuck them up in bed and go out of the room. And start again the next night.

We are conditioned up to the age of seven years old. We absorb information like a sponge in the Theta child's mind. We go from Theta to Alpha to Beta after seven years, when we advance, develop, and learn through repetition.

So while a child is sleeping, they are in delta, which is sleep mode, and by being persistent and getting their little finger to respond to you, they are open to suggestions and have gone from delta to theta, which means they are now in a very deep state of hypnosis. Any suggestion given will take root in their subconscious mind and be acted upon.

Do this for 30 days.

Chapter 25: Reprogramme the Child's Mind

Now let us reprogramme a child's mind. Originally this was put in my first book, Are You Reliving Someone Else's Life? But I want to include this here because I feel this is important for your child.

How to reprogram a child's mind?

Simply put, when we go through something over and over again, it sticks with us. It also becomes second nature the more we do it.

Before the age of seven, our minds are like a sponge, in the Theta state of development, and we are effectively "programmable." At age seven, our brain waves shift from Theta to Alpha and Beta, where we continue to mature and learn through habitual practice.

We have two opportunities each day to rewire our brains; right before we drift off to sleep at night and when we first open our eyes in the morning. We have returned to the Theta state (the state of mind possessed by a child) at this time. At this moment, our thoughts become our reality.

Repetition is the key.

"30 Days working on one problem at a time."

The mind does not know what is real and what is not. When our conscious mind conflicts with our imagination, imagination always wins.

This daily procedure is so crucial that it cannot be skipped.

Every night when they are asleep, and first thing in the morning before waking up, play an audio recording. The recording discusses the aspect of your situation that you wish to alter for your child.

Your own personal "30 Days working on one problem at a time". You will need the use of isolating headphones, or ones that cancel out external sounds.

If you want to train your child's brain, he or she will listen to the audio link below. For the next 30 days, place headphones on your child and allow them to listen to this recording when they're asleep in bed, and then first thing in the morning before they wake up. For the next 30 days, focus solely on the one single thing you want to alter.

So when your little one is fast asleep you place headphones on your child, press play, and when it's finished turn the recording off and take the headphones off.

Remember, 30 days.

Here is the link: https://www.inheritedtherapy.com

This is a recording that will explain in detail how to make the recording for your child.

It is also important that you listen to any recording that you have bought elsewhere first, to make sure it is safe for your child. I would recommend making the recordings yourself. The only one who understands your child is you. They need encouragement and love from their parents

What if you feel that, after these approaches, your child needs more help?

Chapter 26: The Loveday Method for Children

There is another solution for your children. The use of Inherited Therapy and The Loveday Method.

A passage from my book, Are You Reliving Someone Else's Life.

"Chapter 33: Inherited Therapy and The Loveday Method with the use of hypnosis.

"Inherited Therapy is a new approach to helping people release this invisible force controlling people's lives today.

"Just suppose you could access a part of the brain and navigate through the mind to relive the feelings and emotions of our ancestors and experience what they felt and how their life's journey affects our life today and give them back.

"To be able to take you on a journey where you will relive a moment in the first person as your

grandfather, grandmother, uncles, or aunts and let go of the traumas you have been holding.

"And that we are reliving someone else's life."

The Loveday Method is a sophisticated means of achieving time travel through the mind to access hidden memories within the DNA responsible for generational trauma, to unlock the shackles your ancestral traumas hold over you.

This is a programme of six sessions which is custom made for each individual, both adults and children.

Why do we do six sessions you may ask?

Professor Alfred A. Barrios, PhD, surveyed the relevant literature and found the following recovery rates:

- Psychoanalysis: a success rate of 38% after 600 sessions;
- Behaviour Therapy: a success rate of 72% after twenty-two sessions;

Hypnotherapy has a success rate of 93% after just SIX sessions.

You should now be able to see how successful hypnotherapy is. But this is Inherited Therapy, and I feel the success rate is closer to 98%.

But, no guarantee can be given. The results can vary from person to person. But over the Covid period, I worked with approximately 200 clients on Zoom, using these same techniques, and the results were mind-blowing.

These techniques are tested every day. The journey you are taking, you will not believe unless you have experienced it for yourself. It is Magical.

I mentioned six sessions; well, there are seven. The first session is the pre-talk. This session is free.

During the pre-talk, a comprehensive discussion of the client's past will take place. After hearing the pre-talk, it will become abundantly clear to you that the emotions you have been clinging to were present long before you were even born.

Following the pre-talk, if you believe it is for you and you want our help, appointments will be scheduled; otherwise, there will be no charge.

When working with children up to the age of 18 a parent will be present.

And so the journey begins. Over six weeks, one session per week.

There you have it, the help your children desperately need is here.

For information visit these sites.
https://www.inheritedtherapy.com
https://www.liverpoolhypnosis.co.uk

The Journey

Session 1

In the first session we work on the human mind of the present and the memories, by a gentle approach using regression, the child's emotions will be brought to the surface to face the problem.

During that session they will be shown unconditional love by taking them back to the first time they walked, their first birthday, when they were born when their mum is healthy the child is healthy and the mother held the child in her arms for the first time, they will be taken into the mother's womb they will feel a connection of what the mother was going through and the feelings she felt well before the child was born.

You have to understand that it feels real. They see and hear everything. After that, they will be taken to happy times in that child's life.

Now depending on the age of the child ranging from 11 to 18 years, also with the parent's consent, when a child has lost a family member, it can have a huge effect on the child as they go through life. They can be taken to see them, release these feelings and give them back. I must emphasise that the parent has to give their permission. I am not a medium, I am a guide. The parent will always be present.

They are then brought out of hypnosis. The first session can be emotional. During the 48 hours following the session, the mind processes and releases, and after that, you will see changes. However, every child is different. And I must stress, no guarantee can be given. The results may vary from child to child. But the results can also be mind–blowing.

Session 2

Your child will be taken on a magical adventure through time and space into the universe, transported to a place of calmness where the veil has been lifted and they can look back through time and see past ancestors, where the problem originated, and release them. They will then be taken to a magical place where we will open up all the chakras in the body.

The session ends; brought out of hypnosis. The changes can be quite remarkable.

Session 3

Wow, what a journey your child will go on now! They are taken to the Akashic library, The Library of Life, and what a journey it is. In this library, they will be transported through time to be able to lead them on an adventure where they can experience something from the perspective of an ancestor such as a grandparent, great–grandparent, uncle, or aunt, thereby releasing whatever traumatic memories they may be clinging to, which has been the cause of the problem they have been holding onto and give them back.

They will be then taken back to the library where they will find the answers they need. I am only a guide. I do not offer them the solutions; they must discover them on their own.

The hypnosis session ends.

Session 4

The next adventure your child will go on is quite surreal. They will be taken on a journey where your child will search for a treasure map. Again they will be transported through time, where they will live a moment in first person as an ancestor many years before they were born. And be able to let go. Of course, there is a lot more but that is the magic.

Session 5

An adventure of change, and the lost key. Next, your child will go on an adventure across time and space to retrieve the misplaced key. After that, they will be transported back in time to a significant event in their past that is the source of a problem in their present life.

Session 6

The magical crystal. Your child will go on a quest to find the magic crystal. A magical gem is the key to your child's past and awaits them on an adventure they must undertake. Their pent-up emotions will finally be released. And so the magic of life begins.

Conclusion

As a parent, you must determine which course of action will provide your child with the greatest benefit. Counselling, cognitive behavioural therapy (CBT), etc.

The medical route can have implications. Medication and the side effects it can have later in life. However, I am in no way implying that in certain cases they are not needed.

It is your decision, of course.

Do hypnotherapists have the answer? We have AN answer. Is it guaranteed? Of course not, do Doctors guarantee? No, they do not.

The hypnotherapist is neither trained in mental health nor a medical practitioner. At no time will the Hypnosis Practitioner attempt to provide medical or mental health therapy.

Approaching feelings or thoughts that the child has tried not to think about for a long time may be painful. I understand that hypnotherapy has potential emotional risks.

But let's be honest, crossing the road has a potential risk.

But these feelings are already there in your child, they are already hypnotised with sadness, fear, unhappiness and worry, our job is to take them out of THAT hypnosis. And give them back their life.

The thing is, you would not be reading this book unless you were looking for help for your child, and searching for answers.

No doubt you have been to doctors, been referred to counsellors, and even been offered medication. And yet your child is still in this dark place and needs help.

Where do you go from here? Remember there is always hope, and people who care. When you combine Inherited Therapy with The Loveday Method, you'll be astounded by the outcomes.

The next step is to speak to one of our dedicated practitioners who have been trained by me in Inherited Therapy and The Loveday Method.

There you have it, the help your children desperately need is here.

For information visit these sites.
https://www.inheritedtherapy.com
https://www.liverpoolhypnosis.co.uk

Or contact me on: geof@inheritedtherapy.com

"Is It Possible To Communicate With The Dead?"

Look out for my next book, the Third in the series of Seven, Coming Out in September 2023.

So come with me, and let me take you on a magical journey to see your loved ones who have passed on; who will live on in your heart forever; gone but not forgotten.

A Journey You Will Never Forget.

Bibliography

1. Wolynn, M., 2017. It Didn't Start with You. Penguin Publishing Group, p.125.
2. https://digital.nhs.uk/news/2018/one-in-eight-of-five-to-19-year-olds-had-a-mental-disorder-in-2017-major-new-survey-finds
3. https://www.aacap.org/AACAP/Families_and_Youth/Facts_for_Families/FFF-Guide/Understanding-Violent-Behavior-In-Children-and-Adolescents-055.aspx
4. https://www.sciencealert.com/mothers-more-likely-to-transmit-anxiety-disorders-to-daughters-than-sons.
5. https://www.ncbi.nlm.nih.gov/pmc/articles/PMC3500267/#:~:text=In%20the%20medical%20literature%2C%20the,survivors%20had%20settled%20%5B4%5D.
6. Yehuda, R., & LeDoux, J. (2001). The neurobiology of fear conditioning: Implications for posttraumatic stress disorder. Journal of Clinical Psychiatry, 62(Suppl 3), 22-31.
7. Miller, E. K., & Rasmussen, A. (2006). Transgenerational effects of the September 11th terrorist attacks. Journal of Traumatic Stress, 19(5), 727-736.
8. https://en.wikipedia.org/wiki/Masaru_Emoto
9. A similar story is taken from the book, Hypnotherapy, by Dave Elman, on pages 67 and 68.
10. https://plato.stanford.edu/entries/descartes/
11. https://www.fi.edu/laureates/marvin-minsky
12. https://en.wikipedia.org/wiki/%C3%89mile_Cou%C3%A9
13. Hypnotherapy by Dave Elman: Book Chapter 22 Page 274. Hypnosis Attached To Sleep. Sleep Hypnosis.

www.ingramcontent.com/pod-product-compliance
Lightning Source LLC
Chambersburg PA
CBHW030254100526
44590CB00012B/395